Checking Out with the Payment Request API

A Practical Introduction to the HTML5 Payment Request API using Real-world Examples

Alex Libby

Apress®

Checking Out with the Payment Request API

Alex Libby
RUGBY, UK

ISBN-13 (pbk): 978-1-4842-5183-6   ISBN-13 (electronic): 978-1-4842-5184-3
https://doi.org/10.1007/978-1-4842-5184-3

Managing Director, Apress Media LLC: Welmoed Spahr
Acquisitions Editor: Louise Corrigan
Development Editor: James Markham
Coordinating Editor: Nancy Chen

Cover designed by eStudioCalamar
Cover image designed by Freepik (www.freepik.com)

Distributed to the book trade worldwide by Springer Science+Business Media New York, 233 Spring Street, 6th Floor, New York, NY 10013. Phone 1-800-SPRINGER, fax (201) 348-4505, e-mail orders-ny@springer-sbm.com, or visit www.springeronline.com. Apress Media, LLC is a California LLC and the sole member (owner) is Springer Science + Business Media Finance Inc (SSBM Finance Inc). SSBM Finance Inc is a **Delaware** corporation.

For information on translations, please e-mail rights@apress.com, or visit http://www.apress.com/rights-permissions.

Apress titles may be purchased in bulk for academic, corporate, or promotional use. eBook versions and licenses are also available for most titles. For more information, reference our Print and eBook Bulk Sales web page at http://www.apress.com/bulk-sales.

Any source code or other supplementary material referenced by the author in this book is available to readers on GitHub via the book's product page, located at www.apress.com/9781484251836. For more detailed information, please visit http://www.apress.com/source-code.

Printed on acid-free paper

*This is dedicated to my family, with thanks for their love
and support while writing this book.*

Table of Contents

About the Author

Alex Libby is an A/B testing developer and seasoned computer book author, who hails from England. His passion for all things open source dates back to the days of his degree studies, where he first came across web development, and has been hooked ever since. His daily work involves extensive use of JavaScript, HTML, and CSS to manipulate existing web site content; Alex enjoys tinkering with different open source libraries to see how they work. He has spent a stint maintaining the jQuery Tools library and enjoys writing about open source technologies, principally for front-end UI development.

About the Technical Reviewer

François-Denis Gonthier is a graduate of the Université de Sherbrooke computer science program. He made his first steps on the work market working for a start-up company delivering cryptographic software using open source technologies. From this point on, he has never strayed far from the Linux and open source world, without really settling in a single area. He went from programming front ends in Javascript and HTML 5.0 to coding web site back ends using Java, J2EE, JSF, or plain old Unix daemons. The cool Web 2.0 kids would call this being a "full stack developer." Nowadays, he mostly works on embedded Android projects and writes Javascript running on Node.js when he's not doing that.

Acknowledgments

Writing a book can be a long but rewarding process; it is not possible to complete it without the help of other people. I would like to offer a huge vote of thanks to my editors – in particular Nancy Chen and Louise Corrigan; my thanks also to François-Denis Gonthier as my technical reviewer and James Markham for his help during the process. All four have made writing this book a painless and enjoyable process, even with the edits!

My thanks also to my family for being understanding and supporting me while writing – I frequently spend lots of late nights writing alone, so their words of encouragement have been a real help in getting past those bumps in the road and producing the finished book that you now hold in your hands.

Introduction

Checking Out with the Payment Request API is for people who want to quickly create checkouts natively in the browser, without the need for extra libraries or costly subscriptions to checkout form providers.

First introduced in 2016, the Payment Request API is designed to allow developers to create checkout forms natively in the browser. It provides a simple, clean interface that presents a consistent user experience, leaving developers to focus on the mechanics of hooking in functionality such as payment methods or authorization providers.

Over the course of this book, I'll take you on a journey through using the API, showing you how easy it is to quickly create checkout forms quickly and easily, with the minimum of fuss – we'll focus on topics such as setting up a basic form, tying in payment methods, dealing with shipping or different currencies, and more, with lots of simple exercises to help develop your skills using the API as a tool.

Checking Out with the Payment Request API is for the web site developer who is keen to learn how to quickly create checkout forms rapidly, without the need for extra libraries or costly checkout services. It's perfect for those who are in Agile teams, where time is of the essence and where developers can produce reusable code that makes use of the API within their chosen framework or development process.

CHAPTER 1

Introducing the API

Let me start with some simple facts:

- $4,574 billion, by the end of the year 2022.

- Over 65% of users are accessing the Internet via a mobile device, compared to just 15% from a desktop.

- The top three ranking web sites (Apple.com, JD.com, and Amazon.com) accounted for over $113 billion sales in 2018...yet the average online conversion rate for desktop users is around 3%, with mobiles weighing in at just over half this value at 1.6%.

Ouch – this sure makes for sobering reading! Hopefully this got your attention – anyone reading these facts should be left in no doubt that shopping online is rapidly overtaking visits to brick-and-mortar stores and that this will just increase over time. There is one fact though that will bring this into context and might help explain why these numbers are not higher: a study run by Google found that over 65% of people who purchase using a mobile device will stop part way through a purchase.

Why? Well there are a number of reasons for this – a classic example is a process that is too long (on average, this can be as many as 15 steps), or the web site crashed with errors. Shipping charges has been cited as another reason, along with difficulties in entering information or the need to have to create an account before making a purchase.

You can see more figures in detail at www.cpcstrategy.com/blog/2018/11/mcommerce-statistics/, https://baymard.com/blog/checkout-flow-average-form-fields and https://blog.globalwebindex.com/trends/device-usage-2019/.

© Alex Libby 2019
A. Libby, *Checking Out with the Payment Request API*, https://doi.org/10.1007/978-1-4842-5184-3_1

We clearly need a different approach – browser vendors have tried to solve this with various autofill options, but these are not perfect and can end up with us entering incorrect information. Service providers have also played a role too – there is a healthy selection of shopping carts available, but many require you to sign up for a service, or lock you into a single provider, which will cause issues in the event of service failure. Question – is there any alternative available?

Anyone remember the days when shopping carts (and payment options) first became available for online sites? This has mushroomed into a healthy industry, with the likes of heavyweights such as Actinic or Shopify being popular choices for many site owners.

However, these come at cost – not only do we have to pay for licensing but also allow for support (and yes, software is never infallible!). There is also the matter of size – these heavyweights may work well for larger sites, or where there is a good range of products, but will be overkill for smaller outfits. In an age where simplicity is king, we need an alternative: let me introduce you to the Payment Request API!

First introduced in early 2016, the Payment Request API is an emerging standard being developed by the W3C in an attempt to simplify the payment process. Although the look may vary between browsers, it was designed to provide a consistent approach that is available natively in the browser - we can see an example of this in Figure 1-1:

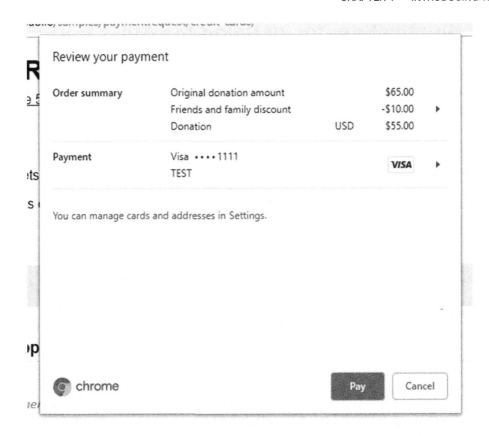

Figure 1-1. *An example of the Payment Request API in action in Chrome*

It removes the need for big bulky carts and payment options and allows us to design simpler, more efficient payment options that tie in to the cart. The latter is great, as although we will need to subscribe to payment providers, the built-in cart contains a mechanism which makes it simpler to hook different payment providers into a common interface. This is something we will begin to explore in more detail from Chapter 2 onward, but for now let's dive in and take a look at the benefits of using the Payment Request API in more detail.

Exploring the Benefits of Using the API

As with any new technology, I am sure that one of the first questions you will ask is – how will it benefit me, my customers, and ultimately, my business? Well, there are a number of reasons why the API should be considered:

- From a customer perspective, it makes for a vastly simplified flow through the site, using details already stored in the browser with just a few clicks (or taps), instead of having to enter them manually, which can be a real pain particularly on small mobile devices!

Creating a one-click type purchase route was patented by Amazon – this was worth $2.4 billion annually in terms of revenue; now that this patent has expired, it's open to anyone to replicate it, which is easy to do with the Payment Request API.

- Making use of the Payment Request API allows payment handlers and service providers to create different types of payment options which are easier to integrate into the browser, can be more secure (with fewer points of failure), and ultimately help better serve customers.

- Implementing the API makes it easier for merchants to set up a variety of different payment options that use the same common interface, instead of having to create ones which are bespoke and might conflict with others.

If an option can help make our service offer easier to use for customers, then clearly it is something we should consider! This is borne out by three key principles that are the underlying foundation of the API:

- It's **easy and consistent** to use – Web Payments store payment and address details in the browser, which removes the need for customers to fill out forms manually. These details are stored locally in the browser; as the UI is implemented natively, customers will see a familiar and consistent checkout experience, on web sites that implement the API.

- The API is **standard and open** – gone are the days of closed source or proprietary software; the API is an open standard for the Web that can be implemented and modified as needed by developers.

- The API is also **secure and flexible** – this second principle is based on using industry-leading payment technology to the Web, which can easily integrate a secure payment solution.

This makes the API an even more attractive offer – we live in times where customers are demanding easy to use sites that offer a simple and consistent experience, so implementing the API is almost becoming essential! Okay, that comment was probably a little biased, but anything that offers a better level of transparency, speed, and simplicity for our customers should be at the top of the list for consideration.

Breaking Some Common Misconceptions

Hopefully by now I've piqued your interest, and that you're all ready and raring to learn more about what the API can offer, right? There's certainly much more to cover – we're only just getting started....

Before we go any further though, I have a small confession to make: I have to shatter a few home truths! Yes, some of you might have read ahead, and formed certain – shall we say expectations? – about what the API means for your site. I suspect some will be misconceived though, so without further ado, let's take a look at some of what those misconceptions are, and see what it means for us in reality:

- Some of you may be worried about how well it handles different types of payments, right? You need not fear – the API is designed to be an open standard that can handle pretty much any type of payment, such as points, e-money, or even bank transfers. If it doesn't work in the API, then it's very likely that support has not been set up, and not that it "works better or worse than other methods."

- I suspect a good number of you may be thinking that once the API is implemented, then you don't have to do anything about processing payments, or ensuring your site is PCI compliant, right? Well, I hate to disappoint on both counts, but you as a developer will still need to implement both! Remember – the API is about providing a simple, consistent experience for your customers; treat it as a replacement for the checkout form you might have otherwise used. You will still need to ensure payments are processed correctly, and that your site is PCI compliant.

We'll revisit the subject of security later in this chapter.

- Hands up anyone who has done a quick Internet search, and come across terms such as "Google Pay", "Apple Pay", and the like? Well, we can make use of them in our cart, but it's important to distinguish that these are not the Payment Request API but the payment providers that hook into our new cart.

It's important to make sure we set clear expectations, and appreciate that the API is not some silver bullet that will auto-magically create the perfect experience for us; it's a good step in the right direction that allows us to focus on the more important parts such as adding in payment providers. There are still some elements we have to work out (such as totals), but we can rest in the assurance that we're not having to develop something really complex that is super complicated to manage and support!

Okay – let's move on: now that we've been introduced to the API and learned something of the benefits of using it, let's turn our attention to something a little more in-depth: some of the terminology used when working with the API. Over the course of this book, we'll cover a number of key terms that relate to different processes or features within the API; let's take a moment to meet them for the first time.

Understanding Terminology Around the API

Over the last few pages, we've covered how the API was designed to be an open, transparent standard, into which we can connect all manner of different payment types. I also mentioned the likes of Google Pay, Apple Pay, and so on – how do all of these fit together?

Well, it's very straightforward – although there will be a fair amount of (two-way) traffic, the API is just one part of the Web Payments standard:

- **Payment Request API (PR API)** – this provides a fast, efficient, and consistent checkout through a native browser UI while at the same time reducing the need to enter shipping and payment details at every visit.

- **Payment Handler API (PH API)** – when using the API, we can configure any number of web-based payment applications that act as payment methods, using the Payment Handler API. These are all provided via a common interface, which reduces the complexity around building payment options into the checkout process.

- **Payment Method Manifest** – this acts as the reference book for each payment method; it defines how it works and participates in the payment ecosystem.

- **Payment Method Identifiers** – these let us define how strings are used to identify each payment method, such as Google Pay, credit cards, and the like. These allow anyone to create their own payment method that can use URL-based payment method identifiers.

To put this into context, there are four players – we have **customers**, who use the checkout process to purchase items. These are made available for sale on sites operated by **merchants** and processed by the appropriate **payment service providers (PSP)**, based on payment handlers specified in the checkout process. We can see how these all fit together in Figure 1-2.

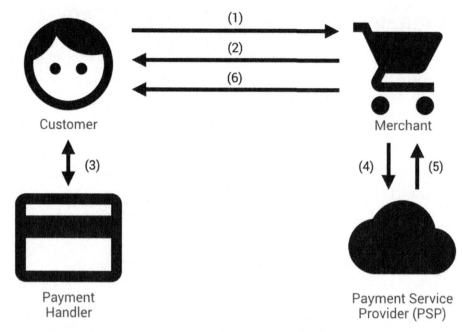

Figure 1-2. *The Payment Request API process explained*
Source: Google.com

Although there are only four key entities to any transaction that involves the Payment Request API, there are nevertheless some important actions that take place between each entity.

1. At the point of purchase, the merchant presents a payment request to the customer in the form of the Payment Request API, using one of the various payment methods specified by the payment method handlers.

2. This can include credit card details saved in the browser or payment handlers such as Google Pay, Alipay, or Samsung Pay. At this point, the merchant can also request shipping details and the customer's contact information.

3. At the point the customer chooses their preferred method of payment – this might be saved credit card details or a web-based payment app such as Google Pay. After the customer authorizes the payment, the payment handler returns a response to the Payment Request API, which relays it to the merchant site. (If the payment is push type such as bank transfers or cryptocurrencies, the payment is already processed when the merchant receives the response.)

4. The merchant site sends a payment credential to a PSP to process the payment, initiates funds transfer, and verifies the payment on the server.

5. The PSP then processes the payment, by securely requesting a funds transfer from the customer's bank or credit card issuer to the merchant; it then returns a success or failure result to the merchant web site, based on the outcome of processing the payment.

6. The merchant web site notifies the customer of the success or failure of the transaction and displays the next step, for example, shipping the purchased item.

Now that we've covered the basic mechanics of the API, let us turn our attention to how we should create a seamless experience for our customer. It has to be said that there are still limits on what we can achieve using the Payment Request API; this said, there are still some pointers we should consider, so let's take a look at what is involved in more detail.

Considering the UX Experience

Up until now, we've focused at a high level on some of the key technical terms and principles that are associated with the API; it is important to also consider the UX experience for our users.

The Request Payment API is made up of two key UX elements. They are known as the **receipt view** and the **edit view**, with an example of the former shown on the left in Figure 1-3, and the edit view demonstrated on the right.

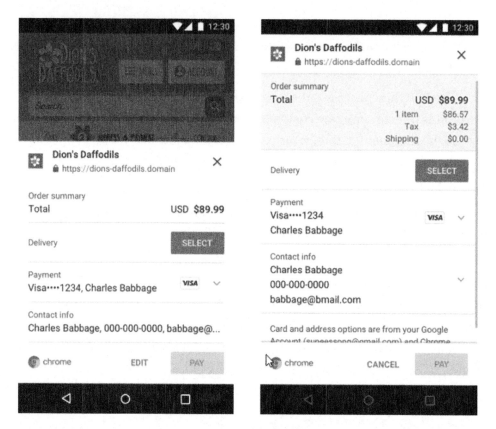

Figure 1-3. *The receipt and edit views in the API*
Source: Google.com

The receipt view affords the customer a chance to take a look at their payment details, with the option to edit each as necessary, against each section. When the customer taps (or clicks on) any of the call to actions from the receipt view, we enter the edit view which will fill the screen and takes over the journey.

Although we've talked about the experience from a mobile perspective, the same concepts apply for those accessing the API from a desktop PC.

Looking further afield, our number one priority must of course be to provide a seamless experience for our customers, that keeps them coming back for more – with this in mind, we should absolutely explore what the Payment Request API means in terms of the UX experience for visitors to a site.

We may not be able to customize it completely (yet), but we can at least effect some changes to help tailor the experience for our customers. Before we do so though, let's start with exploring some typical checkout flows, so we can see at what point the Payment Request API fits into the overall flow of our checkout process.

Exploring Checkout Flows

When using the Payment Request API, it's important to understand the checkout flow – customers are fickle creatures, and not everyone will want to follow the same path to our checkout! So, what does this mean for a Payment Request API-enabled cart?

When a customer selects an item and clicks on Buy, on a Payment Request API-enabled checkout, they enter the checkout flow, and the browser takes over. If details have already been entered (such as payment or shipping options), then these will be displayed by default, or customers can enter them if appropriate.

I would also recommend mapping out the user flow for each way that the customer can get to the checkout. This is something we'll explore further toward the end of the chapter, but in summary, the common entry points that we would need to design for are

- The user is immediately directed to checkout.

- The user starts at the home page, views their cart, and is directed to checkout.

- The user starts at the home page, looks at an item, and is directed to buy now.

- The user starts at the home page, clicks to add an item to their cart, and is directed to checkout.

- The user starts at the item and is directed to the checkout.

A visual representation though is clearly far more useful – for this we can use an application such as Sketch (for MacOS), or Lunacy for those of you using Windows. It's a perfect opportunity for us to get started with something practical, so without further ado, let's take a look at what's involved in creating a sketch diagram of an example flow through an e-commerce web site.

Sketching a User Flow Using Sketch

For the purposes of this exercise, we'll use Lunacy, as this runs on the platform used by the author; the look and feel may be different, but the principles will still be the same. Before we get stuck in though, we need to avail ourselves of some icons – for this exercise, you will need the following:

- House

- Empty cart

- Cart with plus sign

- Eye

- Credit card

- Group of people

- Down-facing triangle

There are plenty of online sites with icons you can download – as a start, try out www.flaticon.com or https://icons8.com. Assuming we have the icons downloaded, let's make a start on our exercise:

USING LUNACY TO DRAW AN EXAMPLE FLOW

1. We'll begin by downloading and installing Lunacy – head over to https://icons8.com/lunacy, then click the Windows Installer link to download the setup file.

2. Once downloaded, double-click the file to begin the installation – for the purposes of this exercise, accepting the defaults will be sufficient.

3. Next, go ahead and fire up the application – look for the mountain icon on the left of the main drawing area; this is to add in images to our image.

4. Click this image, then select the Group of People icon we saved at the start of this exercise – go ahead and position this to the top center of the drawing area. This represents the customers to our site.

5. Next, we need to draw a five-way split, to represent the different routes to the checkout – for this, we can use the Line tool (two up from the Image tool in the toolbox). Click this, then draw a five-way split, like an organigram – we should start to see something like the screenshot shown in Figure 1-4.

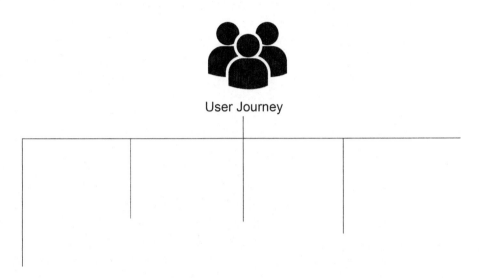

Figure 1-4. *A (part) completed flow diagram*

6. Next, go ahead and add an instance of your Home icon – put this at the bottom of the **second from left** line; this route represents those who start at the home page, then go to the cart before checking out from the site.

7. Repeat step 6, but this time put the icons at the bottom from the middle line and the second from right line.

Using the same principles from the last few steps, we can create our example flowchart to look like the one shown in Figure 1-5 (shown overleaf).

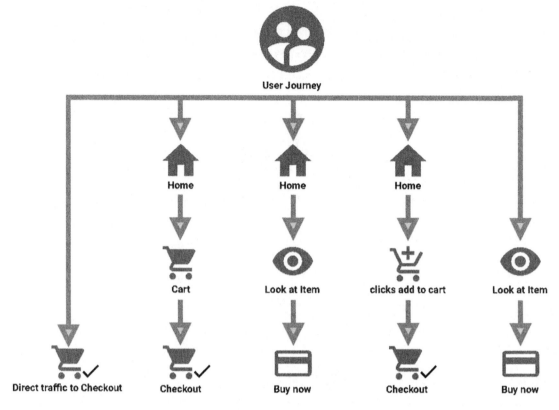

Figure 1-5. *Our completed mock-up of the purchase process*

Once we've created our diagram, we can export the content easily – to this, follow these steps:

8. Use your mouse to select all of the elements on the page, then select the Export tab on the right.

9. In this tab, select Local files then 1x as the size and format and SVG as the image format. Make sure also that As a single image is also selected.

Note   You will see an option to select PNG; it's worth noting that there have been issues with how these display in some instances, hence the reason for selecting SVG. SVG gives the added benefit of allowing elements to be restyled if needed.

---

10. Click Export Object, then choose a suitable location to store the exported image which you can then open in a browser to view the results.

Although it takes a little practice, it is nevertheless a useful tool that we can use to mock up the various routes that customers can take to get to our checkout.

This is not the only way we can use it – google has created a stickersheet with the various elements that make up the Payment Request API, such as the buttons, shipping section, labels for displaying the total amounts, and the like. It means we can mock up what our final payment request will look like; it's worth noting though that although we can't change the layout (such as moving shipping below taxes), we can at least see how it will look when developing any project that makes use of the Payment Request API.

You can see more details and download the stickersheet at `https://bit.ly/ 2JIn9Y7`.

Irrespective of how we design our checkout flow, the one thing we should absolutely not do is to block a purchase when using the API – if we're on a browser that does not yet support it, then we should fall back to an alternative checkout process rather than generate an error message.

Assuming we now have a handle on how our checkout process flows, we can now turn our attention to customizing that experience. At this stage we shouldn't limit ourselves to just changing labels and the like in the cart – there is a host of other things we can do, so let's dive in and take a look at how we can improve the experience for our customers.

Customizing the UX

It's important to understand at the outset that although the Payment Request API was designed to provide a consistent look and feel across all browsers, you might be forgiven for thinking that at first glance the same checkout may *look* different.

This is just down to how the API has been implemented in each browser, and that browser vendors have not yet reached a common standard, in much the same way that developers used to have to support vendor prefixes for some other styling attributes such as border-radius.

This said, there are limits on what we are able to customize with regard to the look and feel within the cart – it is possible this might change in future updates to the API, but for now, Figure 1-6 shows the elements we can change.

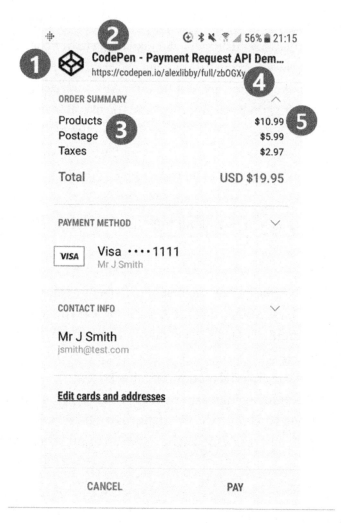

Figure 1-6. *Elements we can customize in the API*

So – what can we change? Let's take a look:

1. The icon at the head of the cart is taken from the site's favicon; this can be a high-resolution image but should be recognizable from within the cart. Ideally, we should provide multiple icons so that the browser can pick the most appropriate one for the available screen estate.

2. The name at the top of the cart is taken from the \<title\> tag of your site, so should include the name of the site in the title.

3. This text label can be modified when constructing the Payments Request API – we'll touch on how, later in Chapter 3.

4. This is the URL of your site.

5. The price and currency are taken from the total specified in the API construct.

Although not displayed as a separate section, we can also modify the shipping label used – this can be selected from a preset list which includes shipping, pickup, or delivery.

The elements highlighted in Figure 1-6 are based on using Chrome. Other browsers may contain different UI elements as well, or even labels for buttons such as "Pay" and "Cancel" – we'll explore this topic further when we come to create our own carts in Chapter 2.

We can, and should, take this further though – the preceding changes are easy to implement, but I always maintain that the mark of a good developer is someone who has an understanding of the bigger picture and not just the technical changes required to configure the API.

I wouldn't expect every developer to be a UX expert at the same time (indeed, you will often find that larger companies have dedicated UX resources for this purpose), but giving some thought to how we link to the API from our shopping cart is a useful skill to have. With this in mind, let's dive in further and take a look at some wider tips we can follow, as a starting point for implementing the API within our site, in more detail.

Some General UX Advice

When it comes to implementing the API within our site, it's easy enough to simply drop it in and not give any thought to the wider picture; we risk missing out on some easy opportunities! To see what I mean, let's take a look at a few low-hanging tricks that are easy to implement, starting with checking small details such as the buttons we use on the site.

Button Design

One of the easiest changes we can make relates to the buttons we use – are they of the right size, for example? There are several avenues we can explore, which include (but are not limited to) the following:

- I would recommend keeping button labels short and aligned to recognizable branding (as indicated in Figure 1-7) – the API is designed to work on different devices where space may be at a premium.

Figure 1-7. *Adding Buy now buttons to create a quick experience*

- When it comes to creating buttons (and particularly ones for launching the API), we should make sure each touch target is wider than the visual element. It's harder to tap a button on a mobile device and get a response if it is very small! For example, if our button were 24 x 24 pixels square, then our touch target should be at least 48 pixels square or larger, depending on the size of the image. I've mocked up an example of how we might show a button in a mobile site, which clearly needs tweaking (Figure 1-8).

Product: Fortissimo
Description: A combination of coffees for a round taste with character.

a.button.see-more | 95.47 × 35

More Details   Add to Cart

Figure 1-8. *Determining the size of our buttons*

Shipping

Once a customer has bought something, we clearly need to arrange delivery – the following list contains a few ideas of what we can easily check and consider fine-tuning for optimal experience:

- When displaying the shipping options, we should also give some context to when purchases will be delivered, if a delivery type is selected (Figure 1-9).

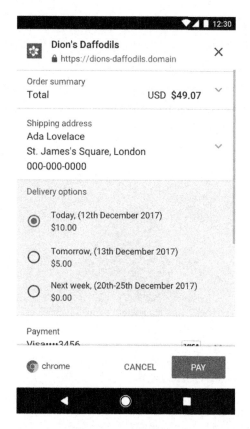

Figure 1-9. *Displaying delivery dates*

This will help give confidence to the customer and reduce the risk of selecting a date when the customer is not able to receive the goods.

- In an ideal world, we would automatically select the customer's default address; it is better practice though to allow them to select it themselves. We then verify that it is correct and adjust what we display as available shipping options (e.g., we don't show international shipping rates if the customer is based in your home country!)

There is a risk with automatically selecting an address – it might be one to which you can't deliver products to, which will only serve to create friction with the customer and potentially result in an abandoned sale.

Navigation

Staying with the theme of making simple changes, another area we can examine is navigation – there are a couple of ideas we can consider:

- Try to eliminate unnecessary steps where possible – keeping the UI simple with clearly labelled Call to Action (CTA) buttons, such as "Add to Cart" or "Download PDF", for a technical schematic download. Taking steps to make it a one-tap purchase and removing the need to have to register will give customers a perceived increase in speed when it comes to checking out. The API was designed with speed in mind, so requesting these pre-saved details from the user will avoid the need to require users to log in to your site.

- I would recommend testing your site under poor network conditions – this will highlight any weak spots where content is not displayed quickly and allow us to improve the checkout flow. A study performed by Google found that 70% of users dropped a sale due to content not rendering sufficiently quickly.

Fallback Options

There may be instances where customers are not able to make use of the Payment Request API, because their browser does not support it; this is becoming less of an issue though, as most mainstream browsers (of the last 2-3 years) support it to some degree. However, for those who still need to use older browsers, there are a couple of points to consider:

- It may seem as if we're doubling up our work, but I would strongly recommend providing a fallback option for customers whose browser does not yet support the API – support is improving all of the time, so this is likely to be a short- to medium-term requirement that can be deprecated once the API is officially supported across browsers. (The only notable exception is Internet Explorer, which has already been superseded by Edge; the latter supports the API).

- For those browsers that do support the API, we will need to adjust the experience for existing, already signed-in customers, to help get them accustomed to the changes. We might, for example, include a button marked "Buy Now" or "Pay with a new card" – this will give these customers an opportunity to start using the API.

Miscellaneous

Last but by no means least are a couple of items to consider – these don't fall into any particular group that we've covered thus far, but should still be explored:

- The choice of language we use when creating CTA buttons is key – it may seem odd to need to consider this, but a small change in text can have a profound effect on overall conversion and ultimately revenue earned from your site. It's also important to ensure consistency, and that your choice makes sense to customers.

- Bear in mind that the API does not deal directly with additional options such as gift cards or loyalty numbers – this is something we will need to factor into any design, to help maintain a seamless experience for our customers.

We'll cover more on this subject in Chapter 3.

Phew – there's a lot to consider there! Many of these tips should be common sense though; we will go through all of these throughout the course of this book, so we can understand what we need to allow for when configuring the API. Before we move on though, there is one more key point we should cover off: feedback to customers! No one likes a system that doesn't tell you what is happening, so what can we do, particularly if space is at a premium?

Giving Feedback Throughout the Journey

Although we've already covered a good handful of ideas, there's always room for one more, and perhaps one of the most important – feedback!

The browser will already handle some aspects of processing each request, but to ensure customers are kept informed, we should signal what is going on at each stage to our customers. This might include:

- Informing the user if their payment has been aborted

- Preparing the user for the checkout process by providing a notice to tell customers that you will be asking for payments

- Signaling to the user that payment was complete and successful

There are plenty of ways to do this, but one we might consider is to use the Snackbar UI approach. People can normally read between 200 and 400 words a minute, so leaving a short message of around 5 words near the foot of the screen will work perfectly, as demonstrated in Figure 1-10.

Figure 1-10. *An example of a Snackbar UI message*

We should provide feedback throughout each stage of the journey – not just to inform if the purchase was successful but also if there are any issues with details entered, such as an invalid date format.

> If you would like to learn more about Snackbar UI elements, then head over to the documentation provided on the Material.io design site at `https://material.io/design/components/snackbars.html#usage`.

Okay – let's change tack and move on: before we do so, there is one topic which should feature at the top of anyone's list. How do we ensure our checkout process is secure? It goes without saying that we as humans always fear what we don't know, but that said, there are a few things we can consider with regard to security, so let's take a look in more detail.

Addressing Security Concerns

With this new API, we should be mindful of security – this is not just at a basic level on the site but also as part of the wider picture with regard to customer transactions. When operating the API, we must maintain a high degree of confidentiality and address any privacy concerns, so that the customers can be confident in using the new technology.

Over time, there will be a number of security issues that are likely to surface, including those that might appear from changes to the API – to get us into the mindset of considering security, let's start with a few pointers that we should consider:

- Our first concern is that of keeping information confidential. We've already talked about how the API must be run in a secure context; it's worth noting that although the API does not directly support encryption of data fields, we can consider encrypting individual fields within payment methods to provide additional protection.

- What happens if we happen to lose a mobile device which has been used to purchase products from sites that use the Payment Request API? Should we consider the device lost and include those credit cards that are saved on the device? In some respects, this is no less secure than carrying the credit card in a wallet – the browser will always ask for a CVC number which won't be present, before a transaction can be authorized.

- The provision of shipping details in a mobile device may be a concern for some, particularly if on a mobile device that is stolen or lost – although purchases cannot be completed without the CVC number, it opens a risk of fraud if someone manages to hack into the phone and can retrieve the details.

- The API states that no details such as shipping address should be shared with any developer, unless the customer has given consent – to help prevent identification of a customer, the API provides an option to limit the details shared to allow a developer to calculate shipping costs or tax information, but not enough to identify that customer.

- Although the API has reached Candidate Recommendation stage, there is still some inconsistency around how details can be stored – for example, Chrome will allow details to be added without the need for a password, whereas Edge requires one before anything can be added or changed.

- When setting up payment methods to service providers, it is common to add these via an iframe in code; this helps to reduce the risk of hacking as the payment method runs in its own environment and is not part of the host site. The Payment Request can also support this option if needed; it has a number of methods which can be called to help ensure that payment requests can be made safely and securely.

I am sure that over time, we will come across other similar concerns – it's only when the API becomes mainstream and we see more widespread support will we likely be more comfortable in using the API. Don't get me wrong – the API is very solid and can absolutely be used now; it is just about making sure that we consider all aspects so that any risks associated with new technologies can be reduced and hopefully eliminated over time!

Summary

Exploring a new API can be a double-edged sword – there is excitement in what we might discover but also a certain amount of trepidation as to what this might mean for our projects and what we must consider in order to make best use of the new feature. Over the course of these pages, we've covered a host of ideas and techniques around the API, as precursor to starting development – let's take a moment to review what we've learned in more detail.

We kicked off with a brief introduction of the API, before swiftly moving on to exploring some of the benefits and misconceptions around this new technology. We then covered off some of the basic principles around the API, before taking a high-level look at mapping out and customizing the API. We then rounded out the chapter with a quick discussion on some of the security concerns that we might face when using the Payments Request API in a production environment.

We've certainly covered a lot of theory; now it's time to take our first steps into developing a solution using the API. It promises to be a real ride, with a lot to cover, so without further ado, we'll begin with looking at the basic code to initiate an API request, in the next chapter.

CHAPTER 2

Setting Up a Basic Checkout

Now that we've been introduced to the Payment Request API, it's time to get stuck into developing code! We've already seen snapshots of what it looks like back in Chapter 1 – before we can get down and dirty with our text editor, there are a few more tools we will need first, in order to complete the exercises in this book.

Some Basic Housekeeping

Before we touch on what we need, there is a key principle I want to share: where possible, we will try to avoid downloading extra tools and make use of what we already have available in our working environment. There's a good reason for taking this approach – I'm a great believer in keeping things simple, and not introducing extra tools unless they are needed. There is a trade-off in taking this approach, where some tasks may not be immediately be possible, but hopefully we can keep this to a minimum.

With this in mind, let's take a look at the tools we need to avail ourselves of, to help set up our working environment. I suspect many of you will already have suitable alternatives in place, so feel free to skip steps if this is the case:

- The most important tool we need is a web server – the API must be run in a secure environment. There are a couple of ways we can achieve this:

    - Use CodePen (`https://codepen.io`), or any available web space if you have as long as it can be secured under HTTPs access.

    - Make use of the local-web-server package which operates under NodeJS (see the next section for details on installing it).

© Alex Libby 2019
A. Libby, *Checking Out with the Payment Request API*, https://doi.org/10.1007/978-1-4842-5184-3_2

- To help store the results of each exercise, I would recommend creating a new folder somewhere on your PC – for the purposes of this book, I will assume you've done this, and that it's called payment. Please alter this accordingly, if you decide to use a different name.

- We of course need a decent text editor – there are plenty of examples available, either as freeware, open source, or commercial offerings. My personal favorite is Sublime Text, available from `www.sublimetext.com/3`; it's a little more expensive than most at $80, but its flexibility is definitely worth the price! You may already have one you prefer to use, so feel free to use that – if not, a good one to try is the cross-platform Atom text editor, available for download from `https://atom.io`.

- As an optional extra, I've also used a font to help provide some visual interest to each demo – it's the Montserrat font, available from the Font Squirrel web site at `www.fontsquirrel.com/fonts/montserrat`. You don't have to include it if you don't want to – the demos will work perfectly fine without it!

Hopefully you've managed to get everything set up, or have suitable tools in place – the key here is that we don't need anything complex when working with the Payment Request API; it's all about simplicity, and working with what works best for your development environment.

For the purposes of this book, I will assume use of both local-web-server for desktop clients and CodePen for mobile browsers; we'll touch on setting up and using both later in this chapter. If you prefer, you can use CodePen throughout.

Setting Up a Suitable Web Server

A key part of implementing the Payment Request API is a need to run it in a secure environment – after all, we're dealing with payment providers, so security is a must!

This may not be an issue on a production web site but isn't so easy when testing locally – fortunately there are several local web servers you can implement using Node.js and NPM. A good example is the `local-web-server` package, available from `https://github.com/lwsjs/local-web-server`; here's how to install it:

INSTALLING NODE.JS AND LOCAL WEB SERVER

For this exercise, I will assume you don't have Node.js already installed – if you do, then please feel free to skip the first two steps:

1. The local-web-server package runs under Node.js, so we must install this first – go ahead and browse to `https://nodejs.org/en/`, then click the LTS option to download an appropriate version for your platform.

2. Go ahead and run the install process – if prompted, please accept all defaults, as this will be sufficient for the purposes of this exercise.

With Node.js installed, we can now go ahead and install our web server, using these steps:

3. Go ahead and fire up a Node.js terminal session – at the prompt, change the working folder to our project folder.

4. Next, enter this command at the prompt, to set up a package manifest file:

    ```
    npm init -y
    ```

5. The resulting manifest will be displayed on screen – at the prompt, enter this command to install our web server:

    ```
    npm install -g local-web-server
    ```

6. When complete, we can now fire up the server – to do this, go ahead and enter this command at the prompt:

    ```
    ws --https --hostname localhost
    ```

7. If all is well, we will see confirmation of the URL it is using to serve content, as shown in Figure 2-1.

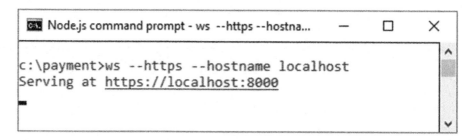

Figure 2-1. *Firing up our web server*

8. Finally, go ahead and copy the index.html file from the setup folder in the code download, to our project area – this we will use to test that the page renders as expected under a secured URL.

If we browse to this URL in Chrome, we would hope to see something – indeed we do, but not before we get this ugly message (Figure 2-2).

Your connection is not private

Attackers might be trying to steal your information from **localhost** (for example, passwords, messages or credit cards). Learn more

NET::ERR_CERT_AUTHORITY_INVALID

☐ Help improve Safe Browsing by sending some system information and page content to Google. Privacy Policy

Advanced   Back to safety

Figure 2-2. *What we see when first browsing our project area...*

Ouch – that's not a great sign! The truth be told is that even though the content is indeed being hosted securely, the certificate we're using can't be independently verified, hence the warning. This is something we can rectify – it does involve a few steps, but fortunately the local-web-server package we're using makes it easier to resolve than had we'd been using a server such as Apache.

At this point I would suggest this is something worth completing – the demo will work without it, but given that most search engines now favor secure content, it seems sensible to replicate this in a local development environment! With that in mind, let's take a look at what is involved in properly securing our demo:

MAKING OUR SITE TRULY SECURE

For the purposes of this exercise, we'll make use of the certificate that is already included within local-web-server. Once configured, this will allow us to browse to `https://localhost:8000` (8000 being the port it uses), without generating a certificate warning in Chrome. We will assume for the purposes of this demo that we are working on Windows (as this is the author's preferred platform) – similar principles though can be used to secure our test area for other browsers.

Please note   These instructions are for setting up a development environment only and should **not** be used for production-facing web sites.

With this in mind, let's make a start:

1. We'll start by firing up the web server in HTTPS mode and browsing to our test site:

   ```
   ws --hostname https://localhost --https
   ```

2. When you see the warning message, click Advanced then Proceed to localhost (unsafe).

3. Press F12 to open Chrome's Developer Tools facility.

4. Next, click the Security ➤ View Certificate ➤ Details.

5. Click Copy to File, then Next, then Cryptographic Message Syntax Standard – PKCS #7 Certificates (.P7B), then "Next" again.

6.   Save the file to the root of our test area for now – it's a temporary measure, to allow us to complete the next step.

7.   Now go ahead and pen Chrome Settings, then search for SSL and click Manage Certificates.

8.   Click Import ➤ Next, then change the file type to PCKS #7 Certificates, and browse to the certificate you exported in step 6. Click Next.

9.   Click "Place all certificates in the following store," then click Browse, and select Trusted Root Certification Authorities.

10.   Click OK if you get a prompt to install the certificate; once you've clicked OK in step 10, then click Yes then OK to accept.

11.   Click Next, Next and Finish, and restart Chrome for the change to take effect.

For those of you using Linux or MacOS machines, you can find similar instructions for enabling SSL support at www.freecodecamp.org/news/how-to-get-https-working-on-your-local-development-environment-in-5-minutes-7af615770eec/. At this point, if we restart our web server and browse to the project site, we should not see a warning – instead, we will see something akin to the screenshot shown in Figure 2-3.

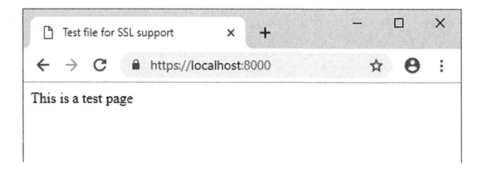

Figure 2-3. *Our project area, properly secured in Chrome*

Okay – enough of the chitchat: it's time for us to get stuck into some coding! The first stage in our discovery of this API is to ascertain which browsers can support it, so without further ado, let's dive in and take a look.

Checking Browser Support for the API

Although support for the Payment Request API is still in a state of flux, it is nevertheless getting better as it edges closer to becoming a mainstream standard.

All of the main desktop browsers have implemented the API in some form – at the time of writing, Safari and Chrome offer the most complete support, with other browsers either missing support for a `retry()` method (7) or requiring visitors to enable support before it can be used. We can see how this shapes up in Figure 2-4.

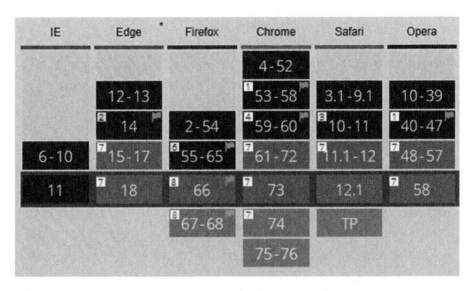

Figure 2-4. *Browser support for the Payment Request API*
Source: CanIUse.com

Now – in this age of mobile device usage, one might hope that support should be at a comparable level, right? A quick check on CanIUse's web site shows otherwise though – support would appear to be very poor! Why might this be, I wonder?

A (partial) reason for this might be due to market share, and that features are unlikely to be developed if usage is low – at the time of writing, CanIUse's web site was reporting that those mobile browsers which don't support it account for less than 6% market share. In comparison, three browsers form the bulk of mobile support for the API – iOS Safari, Chrome for Android, and Samsung Internet – and that this accounts for over 40% of market share.

Ultimately though we should not let this put us off from using the API, particularly in a mobile environment – support is still improving, and with current trends emphasizing the need for speed and simplicity, it is very likely that support will get better over time.

Enabling Browsers to Use the API

Irrespective of which browsers we target, we still need to know how to check that they can support the API – fortunately this is a cinch, and can be achieved with the following code:

```
if (window.PaymentRequest) {
  // We can continue with the Payment Request API
} else {
  // Here we could fall back to a legacy checkout form
}
```

Assuming the browser supports the API and the result of the preceding statement is truthy, then we can implement it; otherwise we will need to fall back to a legacy checkout form.

The use of the latter does raise an important question though – if the future is around using the API, then do we need to implement a fallback mechanism? The answer to this will depend on which browsers visitors to your site use, and that checking your site's analytics will help determine whether there is a need to implement the fallback checkout form.

This is not about limiting which browsers your customers can use to transact with your site but prioritizing the time and resource effort required to develop a solution for those browsers that can support the API.

It's equally important to note that some visitors to your site may use browsers where support is disabled by default but can be can be enabled to allow use of the API. For this, customers will need to change their browser configuration; it is unlikely people will do this unless they know what they are doing! Fortunately the need to do this is diminishing; at present most desktop and and mobile browsers support the API in some form, with only Firefox requiring support to be enabled in its configuration.

For a more in-depth look at how to enable support, search for "browser enable flags" on Google; the article at `www.thewindowsclub.com/about-chrome-flags-config-edge-firefox` is one of many that detail how to enable support in most desktop browsers.

Okay – let's move on: now that we've seen how to test our browsers for support for the API, let's get stuck into developing our first example! For the purposes of this next demo, we'll focus on using desktop browsers; we will cover off what to do with regards mobile devices a little later on in this chapter.

Creating a Simple Example for Desktop Browsers

So far, so we've seen how to check whether our browser supports the API; it's time to get to the core of creating our checkout cart! Over the next few pages, we'll put together a simple demo using CodePen (we'll focus on working locally, later), before we dive into the code in more detail to see how it is all put together.

CREATING OUR FIRST CHECKOUT

Our demo makes use of a single image of chillis, taken from the Pexels stock library site at www.pexels.com/photo/red-chillies-illustration-39390/; I've set this up as a GitHub image, to make it easier to access.

Let's make a start on creating our demo:

1. We'll start by downloading a copy of the code download that accompanies this book – go ahead and save it in our project folder that we created earlier in this chapter.

2. Next, browse to https://codepen.io – we first need to add in our markup. For this, go ahead and open a copy of firstcheckout.html from the code download that we saved in step 1; copy the contents into the HTML pane.

3. If we run the demo by itself, it won't look very pretty – to fix this, let's add in some styling. The code for this can be found in firstcheckout.css; copy the contents into the CSS pane.

4. To make it all work, we need to add in the magic that will display our checkout form – the script code for this is in firstcheckout.js, so go ahead and copy the contents into the JS window.

5.   At this point we everything in place to display our checkout – go ahead and save your work. If you have an account already with CodePen, then go ahead and save it to your account; if you want to save it anonymously, then this is equally fine.

Keep a note of the URL for your CodePen demo – you will need it in the next exercise.

---

6.   With everything saved, we can now preview the results of our demo – go ahead and click the red Buy Chillis button in the main pane; we should see our checkout form appear, as indicated in Figure 2-5.

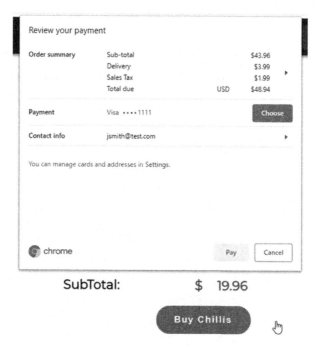

Figure 2-5. *Our first checkout cartGranted, it needs work – it's unlikely at this stage that you will have any details already saved such as credit cards, for example!*

However the basic principles are now in place; we've not needed to create any elaborate carts or spend ages getting it displaying correctly. If we look through the code in more detail, I suspect you might be wondering just what is going on within – don't worry: all will be revealed! The code contains some useful functionality that you will frequently see when working with the API, so let's take a moment or two to explore it in more detail.

Exploring What Happened

If we take a close look at the code in our demo, you might be forgiven for thinking it looks complicated, but in reality, it is simpler than it might appear! The HTML and CSS markup is nothing out of the ordinary, and contains the basic elements you might find when creating a product page (yes, we can add more, but it isn't necessary for the purposes of this exercise.)

Where the fun really starts is in the JavaScript code – let's examine it block by block, to see how it all fits together. We kick off by creating a simple configuration object that defines the payment methods (or payment instruments) for our demo:

```
const methodData = [{
  supportedMethods: 'basic-card',
  data: {
    supportedNetworks: ['visa', 'mastercard', 'amex'],
    supportedTypes: ['credit']
  }
}];
```

We then set up some variables to store a number of values – in this instance, they include both the input box and the value within, along with the subtotal displayed on screen. We then create the (`amount.addEventListener`) event handler to update the subtotal displayed on screen, when adjusting the number of items selected.

Next up comes the core of our code – the event handler that takes care of dealing with clicks on the Buy Chillis button! In this, we start with defining some values for the quantity, subtotal, tax, and shipping costs, before creating an object array that contains the values and labels seen when displaying our cart.

We then get into the real meat of our code – at this point, we specify the options constant, within which we require the customer to enter their email address (`requestPayerEmail: true`). This is then tied together to form a new `PaymentRequest`, before calling it using `request.show` and determining what should happen upon completion or failure.

Okay – let's move on: we have a working cart (of sorts), but it's missing a lot of functionality! How would we deal with errors, for example? What about customers who decide to abort the process? We clearly need something in place to handle these little "bumps," so let's dive in and take a look at how we might implement error checking when using the API.

Managing Errors in the Checkout

In an ideal world, we would expect everything to go smoothly, right? Absolutely...except we live in reality, not something that is a 100% perfect utopia! Mistakes or errors can and do happen – it's up to us as developers to anticipate these possible scenarios and to build in suitable controls to limit or protect the application or web site from falling over into a heap.

So, to ensure our site doesn't completely collapse, what type of errors should we look out for? There are plenty of opportunities that might arise, which might include the following examples:

- The transaction payment fails to complete successfully.

- Selecting an invalid payment method.

- Not listening for changes in shipping, address, or payment (we'll explore shipping in more detail in Chapter 4).

- Customer selects a payment app such as Apple Pay for which they are not registered (we'll explore this more in Chapter 5).

- Timing out due to inactivity.

- Validating fields and failing due to invalid entries.

- Handling unsupported browsers.

In each instance, not only do we need to trap and manage the error but also implement a suitable exit or opportunity to allow the customer to retry the purchase.

If we take a look at the code from our demo in more detail, we can already see a basic level of error trapping in place (as highlighted):

```
        .then(console.log("Payment successful: " + JSON.
        stringify(result)));
}).catch(function(err) {
  console.error(err.message);
});
```

This will trap any errors that occur, but it's not perfect – the response we get back won't distinguish between customers cancelling a valid purchase attempt, against a genuine failure, for example.

We can absolutely improve on this in all manner of different ways; this might be as simple as adding a notification message through to ensuring we select a valid shipping option or ensuring we have entered a valid delivery address. We will revisit this later in Chapter 4 when we explore how to manage shipping; for now (and to give you a flavor of what is possible), we're going to adapt our previous demo to add in some simple error handling.

For our next demo (which comes in three parts), we'll add in some simple messaging, a timeout safety mechanism, and a check to ensure we at least have one method of payment available to us in our checkout form – let's take a look and see what's required to make this happen in more detail.

ADDING SIMPLE ERROR HANDLING

Remember that CodePen demo you created earlier? Well, we need it again – fire it up, before continuing with this exercise:

1. Our first step is to add in a placeholder for our messaging – for this, go ahead and add the following immediately before the closing `</div>` in the HTML pane of our demo:

    ```
    <span id="message"></span>
    ```

2. The first change we will make is to add in functions that will display suitable messaging, depending on the outcome of our transaction. The first one is to confirm a successful transaction – for this, go ahead and add it below the `amount.addEventListener()` event handler, leaving a blank line in-between:

    ```
    function displaySuccess() {
      document.getElementById("message").classList.add("success");
      document.getElementById("message").innerHTML = "<span>\u2714</span>
      Payment received - thanks for your order!";
    }
    ```

You can find the larger JavaScript functions listed in the `errorhandling.js` code file in the accompanying code download, along with the CSS styling in errorhandling.css.

3. The next function will be for those instances where an error or fault appears –
    we hope this is rare, but nevertheless we still have to allow for issues to
    crop up! With that in mind, leave a line, then add this function in below the
    `displaySuccess()` function from the previous step:

```
function displayError() {
    document.getElementById("message").classList.add("failure");
    document.getElementById("message").innerHTML = "<span>\u2716</span>
    There was a problem with payment";
}
```

4. Our third function takes care of those instances where customers have reason
    to abandon the checkout process – for this, add in the following code below the
    `displayError()` function from the previous step:

```
function displayCancel() {
    document.getElementById("message").classList.add("info");
    document.getElementById("message").innerHTML =
    "<span>&#128712;</span>Request has been cancelled";
}
```

5. We have one more ancillary function to add in – this one takes care of
    displaying general messages, not already covered in the previous functions. Go
    ahead and add the following code in, below the `displayCancel()` function:

```
function displayMessage(mesg) {
    document.getElementById("message").classList.add("info");
    document.getElementById("message").innerHTML = "<span>&#128712;
    </span>" + mesg;
}
```

6. Now that we've added in functions to take care of displaying messages, we
    need to add a reset so that when messages are displayed, styling from one
    message doesn't clash with subsequent messages. Go ahead and add the
    following line of code, as indicated:

```
document.querySelector('.pay-button').onclick = function (e) {
    document.getElementById("message").className = ";
    if (window.PaymentRequest) {
```

7. To bring our messaging to life, we need to add in some styling – for this, go ahead and add the following styles in to the CSS pane in our demo:

```
#message { float: left; margin-top: 10px; width: 320px;  display:
none; padding: 10px; font-weight: bold; border-radius: 5px; }
```

```
#message.success { background-color: #ace1af; color: #008000;
  display: block; }
```

```
#message.success > span { float: left; font-size: 30px; color:
#008000; padding: 0px 10px; }
```

```
#message.failure { background-color: #FFD1DC; color: #ff0000;
  display: block; }
```

```
#message.failure > span { float: left; font-size: 30px; color:
#ff0000; padding: 0px 10px; }
```

```
#message.info { background-color: #FCF75E; display: block; color:
#000000; line-height: 20px; }
```

```
#message.info > span { float: left; font-size: 30px; color: #000000;
padding: 0px 10px; }
```

8. Save your demo – we've completed the first part of our changes.

Our next change takes care of adding a check to ensure that at least one method of payment is available for use in our checkout form. First, we're going to take the opportunity to tweak some of the variables in our code, to make them a little more relevant:

1. At the top of our demo, change the const `methodData` = line of code to this:

```
const paymentMethods = [{
```

2. For the payment details block, change this line as indicated:

```
const paymentDetails = {
    total: {
      label: 'Total due',
```

3. On or around line 60 of the JS pane, change the line of text for our payment options to this:

```
const paymentOptions = { requestPayerEmail: true};
```

4. We now need to update our Payment Request object – for this, replace the code
    on or around line 61, with this:

    ```
    let request = new PaymentRequest(paymentMethods, paymentDetails,
    paymentOptions);
    ```

5. Next, remove this block of code – we're going to replace it with an updated
    version that performs the check for the presence of at least one stored method
    of payment being available:

    ```
    //Show the Native UI
    request
      .show()
      .then(function(result) {
        result.complete('success')
          .then(console.log(JSON.stringify(result)));
      }).catch(function(err) {
        console.error(err.message);
      });
    } else {
    // Fallback to traditional checkout
    }
    ```

6. We can now add in our updated event handler that takes care of displaying the
    checkout form – for this, add in the following function, which now includes the
    canMakePayment() check:

    ```
    if (request.canMakePayment) {
        request.canMakePayment().then(function(result) {
          if (result) {
            //console.log(request);
    ```

    This section handles a successful transaction, logging a suitable response to
    console and displaying a customer-friendly message on screen:

    ```
    request.show().then(function(result) {
      result.complete('success').then(function() {
        console.log(JSON.stringify(result));
        displaySuccess();
      });
    ```

In the event we have an issue or the user cancels the request, we handle it gracefully by logging a response to console or displaying confirmation that the request has been cancelled:

```
    }).catch(function(err) {
      if (err.message == "Request cancelled") {
        displayCancel();
      } else {
        console.error(err.message);
displayError();
      }
    });
  } else {
    console.log('Cannot make payment');
    displayMessage("Sorry - no valid payment methods
    available");
  }
}).catch(function(err) {
  console.log(request, err);
});
}
```

7. We're almost done – the last stage is to add in a function to take care of a security timeout; this cancels the process after 20 minutes of inactivity:

```
/* time out requests after 20 mins of inactivity */
  var paymentTimeout = window.setTimeout(function() {
    window.clearTimeout(paymentTimeout);
    request.abort().then(function() {
      document.getElementById("message").classList.add("info");
      document.getElementById("message").innerHTML =
      "<span>&#128712;</span> Request has been timed out due to
      inactivity";
      console.log('Payment timed out after 20 mins.');
    }).catch(function() {
      console.log('Unable to abort, because the user is currently in
      the process of paying.');
    });
  }, 20000 * 60);   /* 20 minutes */
```

8.   Go ahead and save your work – if we preview the form, then hit the Buy Chillis
     button followed by Cancel; we will see the outcome displayed in Figure 2-6.

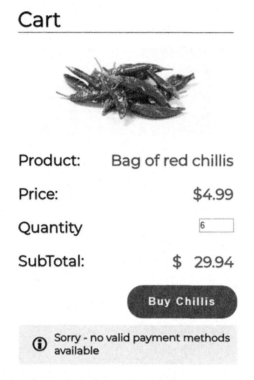

Figure 2-6. *Our demo with updated messaging*

Phew – a fair few changes, even if they were to add in some relatively simple
functionality! We've only touched the surface of what is possible though; we will cover
more options when we visit the subject of adding in shipping in Chapter 4. In the
meantime, our demo covers some key points we should be aware of, so let's dive in and
review the changes we've made to our demo in more detail.

Understanding the Changes to Our Demo

Adding in error handling can open a real minefield of questions – what should we
handle? Is an error something we should allow for, or would we be designing a solution
that in effect encourages bad behavior, for example? That aside, there is some basic
handling we can absolutely include – we've picked up on three relatively simple
examples as our starting point.

We began by adding in a set of functions (and associated styling) to inform customers when a transaction has been successful, has cancelled, or has resulted in a problem. By themselves, these functions are not particularly complicated; they simply render an appropriate message on screen. If we were to optimize our code, these could (and should) be refactored as one generic function – I've written them out in full for clarity in our exercise.

The real magic though happens when we fire the request object in response to clicking the Buy Chillis button – we first trigger `canMakePayment()` to ensure that we have at least one valid method of payment already stored within the browser. The outcome of this (a Boolean value) determines if we then show our checkout cart (using `show()`) or if a lack of payment methods (or instruments) mean we must render a message back to the user to this effect.

Assuming a payment instrument is available, we then `show()` the checkout form; once the customer hits Pay, we trigger `complete()` to determine if the purchase is successful or a failure. We then display the appropriate message – for the purposes of some of the messages, we also log an entry to the browser's console, although you would very likely want to remove this log entry in a production environment.

The third and final part takes care of timing out the basket after 20 minutes, if there has been no activity on the part of the user; we use a standard JavaScript `setTimeout()` function to achieve this, followed by a `request.abort()` method to cancel the process if there has not been any activity.

Adapting for Use on Mobile Devices

In this age of increasing use of mobile devices, we absolutely must consider those customers who prefer not to be tied to a desktop or who might need to order goods remotely (e.g., while on a customer site). Question is: what do we need to do to make our example work on a mobile device?

At this point, I suspect you're probably thinking that we have to change the configuration object defined in the previous exercise, right? Well, I hate to disappoint, but we actually don't have to do anything! Okay – perhaps that is something of a glib response: we don't have to make any changes to the API itself but do need to ensure our styling still works in a mobile context.

To test this, try running the CodePen demo you created in the previous exercise on a cell phone – to get the best effect, I would recommend switching the view to full page view. If all is well, we should see something akin to the screenshot shown in Figure 2-7.

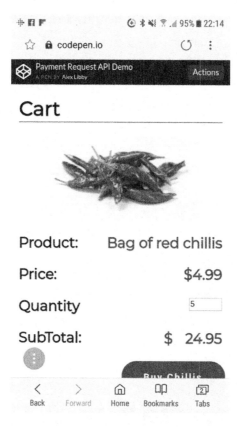

Figure 2-7. *Our example cart shown in mobile format*

In this instance, our example doesn't look materially different – we still have the same elements, although if truth be told, we clearly need to restyle our main call to action, so it fits a little better above the fold!

Where we see the real differences is in the next screen – try tapping on the Buy Chillis button, and we are presented with the same information as before but presented in a format adapted for mobile. Figure 2-8 shows what appears when we run our previous example on a cell phone.

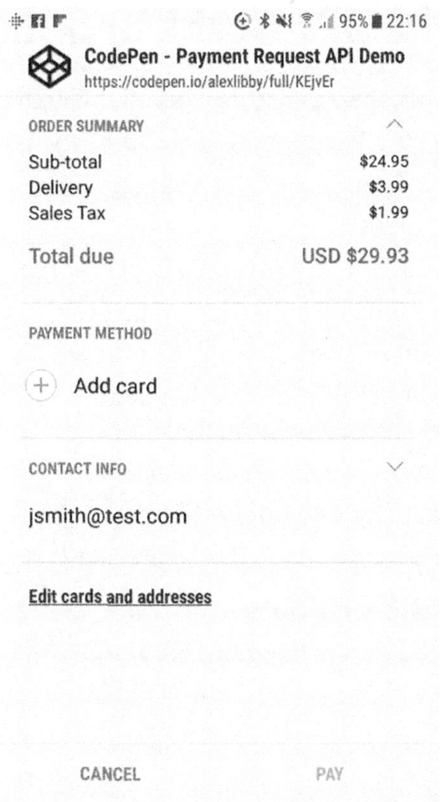

Figure 2-8. *Our demo cart displayed on a mobile device*

The display may look a little different, but the same information is still displayed – there is one key difference though: on a mobile device you may find sections such as the order summary in a collapsed state by default. Other than this, we've not had to make any material changes to how our cart works – indeed, if we'd had to make any, then these would have to have been to styling. If we allow for this during the original design of the site, then we effectively don't have to make any additional changes at all, as the design would allow for both desktop and mobile use.

We're now at a point where we have a basic cart working for both desktop and mobile devices, with a modicum of error handling in place to handle typical errors generated during cart use. We've already explored the code used in this demo, but this only touches the surface of what is possible, so let's take a moment to dive in and explore the API in a wider context, so we can understand more about some of the settings used to configure our demo.

Exploring How the API Works in Detail

Throughout the course of this chapter, we've worked through the steps required to create a basic checkout form using the Payment Request API – the goal being to learn how to quickly and effectively implement the API for your customers, to help create a seamless journey with the minimum of fuss.

Although we can configure the API in a variety of different ways to fit our requirements (such as using Bitcoin, subscription payments, and the like), the basic principle of setting up the API revolves around one statement. To put it into context, we can use the code we created back in the CodePen demo from earlier in this chapter; that statement would be this:

```
const request = new PaymentRequest(paymentMethods, paymentDetails,
paymentOptions);
```

We can specify individual settings for each parameter in turn – using the code from our demo, let's take a look at how each parameter is constructed in turn, beginning with payment methods.

Payment Methods

The first parameter in our PaymentRequest object, paymentMethods, is a list of the payment methods that our site will support, in the form of an array variable. This array is made up of two components – supportedMethods (which is compulsory), plus an optional data property.

It's important to note that we should always specify the basic-card method, which represents standard credit cards and is supported as a standard payment option across all browsers that implement the API. At the same time, we need to also include the supportedNetworks property, which defines the various credit cards that are accepted on our application:

```
const paymentMethods = [{
  supportedMethods: 'basic-card',
  data: {
    supportedNetworks: ['visa', 'mastercard', 'amex']
  }
}];
```

However, this is not the only method we can use – we can add in additional, URL-based, methods such as Google Pay, Alipay, or Apple Pay, using a second instance of the supportedMethods parameter:

```
supportedNetworks: ['visa', 'mastercard', 'amex']
  }, {
supportedMethods: 'https://examplecompany.com/pay
}]
```

These methods only need us to specify the URL to the payment provider's service and do not require any additional data values.

Payment Details

The second parameter, paymentDetails, has to be created as an object and takes care of specifying the payment details for the transaction. For this, we must include as a minimum the total value, which specifies the total payment due from the customer.

The remaining values such as subtotal, shipping, and sales tax are optional and can be specified as needed:

```
const details = {
  total: {
    label: 'Total due',
    amount: { currency: 'USD', value: (subtotal + tax + shipping).
    toFixed(2) }
  },
  displayItems: [{
    label: 'Sub-total',
    amount: { currency: 'USD', value: subtotal.toFixed(2) }
  }, {
    label: 'Delivery',
    amount: { currency: 'USD', value: 3.99 }
  }, {
    label: 'Sales Tax',
    amount: { currency: 'USD', value: tax.toFixed(2) }
  }]
};
```

It's worth noting that although we can specify the currency we're using here, these are just references only; the amount listed is not updated automatically if we had decided to change the currency being used in our demo. For this, we would have to work out the equivalent amount manually in code and post that value instead.

We'll cover the subject of handling different currencies, in Chapter 3.

This is also true of other updates such as displaying discounted prices; although our code includes some basic calculations, the API itself does **not** calculate values. It is up to us as developers to ensure that we pass the correct values into the API at the point of defining the details object. Equally, if we don't include the total value as a required property, this will generate an error similar to the one displayed in Figure 2-9.

```
⊗ Uncaught TypeError: Failed to construct 'PaymentRequest': required     pen.js:43
  member total is undefined.
      at HTMLButtonElement.document.querySelector.onclick (pen.js:43)
```

Figure 2-9. *The error generated when total is missing*

This does not affect the remaining labels that we've added in our demo – these are optional and can be specified as needed in each site.

Payment Options

In comparison, the next parameter, paymentOptions, is a simple object that indicates which payment options a customer has to provide, such as a shipping or contact email address. It takes the following format, where we can specify one or more values:

```
const options = { requestPayerEmail: true };
```

Specifying an email address is not the only option available to us; there are six in total that we can choose to use:

```
var options = {
  requestShipping: true,
  requestPayerEmail: true,
  requestPayerPhone: true,
```

```
  requestPayerName: true,
  shippingType: 'delivery'
};
```

It's important to note that with `shippingType`, we are limited in what can be specified as a title – we can choose to use `shipping`, `delivery,` or `pickup`. It is also case sensitive too; specifying `pickup` as an example will throw the error shown in Figure 2-10.

Figure 2-10. *Specifying an invalid shippingType value*

Although we are limited in what we can pass as a value for shippingType, this does not stop us from specifying something a little more customer-friendly in the label! We might choose to use something like "Delivery" or "Collection," depending on our needs; as long as we pass the correct value for `shippingType`, then it will work fine.

Wrapping it All Together

Now that we've specified each of the settings that we need for our checkout cart, it's time to bring it all together by initiating an instance of our PaymentRequest object, `request`. This creates a Promise as part of a three-step process – the first is to `show()` the checkout form, followed by completing the payment and indicating its success, or switching to the `catch()` statement if it detects a failure or the visitor cancels the request:

```
//Show the Native UI
request
  .show()
  .then(function(result) {
    result.complete('success')
          .then(console.log("Payment successful: " + JSON.
          stringify(result)));
  }).catch(function(err) {
    console.error(err.message);
  });
```

```
} else {
  // Fallback to traditional checkout
}
```

The remaining three lines in bold are not part of the Payment Request execution; these belong to the check we made at the very beginning, to verify that our browser can indeed support the Payment Request API:

```
if(window.PaymentRequest) {

...

} else {
  // Fallback to traditional checkout
}
```

The three sections we've covered, payment details, options, and methods, all of which make up the basic for a Payment Request API call. To fully understand how it all fits together, take a look at Figure 2-11, which shows the various elements of the payment process as a flowchart.

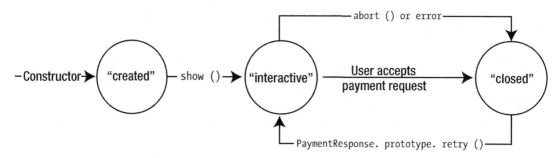

Figure 2-11. *The various code elements of the payment process*

There is a lot more we can add though, such as shipping options, making sure that we handle any changes or errors, and of course integrating the all-important payment processing! We've touched on some of this during the course of this chapter but will expand on this later in the book.

Summary

When one begins to use a new API for the first time, there is always a sense of trepidation – will it work as expected...what support do I need...how does it work? are some of the question we might (rightly) want to ask! Over the course of this chapter we've begun to explore the API for the first time; we've covered some useful techniques, so let's take a few moments to review what we have learnt.

We kicked off our foray into the API with a look at how we can check that target browsers support the API, and what to do for those that don't (such as providing a more traditional checkout form). Next up, we created a basic example of the API as a CodePen demo, with a view to exploring each of the key elements and how they fit together.

We then moved onto understanding some of the errors that might pop up when using the API, before building in some additions to our previous demo to show how this might be achieved. We then explored how the API might work on mobile devices and learned that despite requiring some style changes, the core of the API needed little or no change to work on this platform. We finally rounded out the chapter with a look at the API in detail, revisiting each section of the earlier demo in detail and understanding some of the wider options we can use at this stage in the development process.

Let's get a move on to our next topic: now that we've created our basic example, let's make sure that if our customers change their mind, it will handle and update any changes accordingly. We'll see how, and more, in the next chapter, so hold on tight...!

CHAPTER 3

Configuring and Customizing Our Checkout

Over the course of the previous two chapters, we've been introduced to the Payment Request API and created our first checkout form using the API; if all is well, we now have a basic understanding of how it works and seen how easy it is to create something without the use of additional software...or for that matter, being tied into any ancillary service!

Okay, granted, we would need the latter when it comes to integrating payment providers, but we'd need at least one with a traditional checkout process, so that doesn't count! The key point here though is that we've created something that uses a native feature in more recent browsers (from 2016 onward), using nothing more than a standard text editor.

This aside, we've only scratched the surface of what is possible – now that we have the basics in place, it's time for us to take things further and explore how we can tweak the functionality to our needs. Before we do so, there are two things we should do: the first is to make sure we have a payment method set up. Let's take a look at that first, before setting up our demos locally, so we don't have to rely on CodePen!

Setting Up a Payment Method

If we have to do anything in this chapter, this next step is arguably the most important – we need to make sure we have a valid method of payment set up in our browser.

For the purposes of this book, we'll assume that you're using Chrome – we'll be adding in fake credit card details, so that the forms we develop operate correctly.

© Alex Libby 2019
A. Libby, *Checking Out with the Payment Request API*, https://doi.org/10.1007/978-1-4842-5184-3_3

Let's take a look at what needs to happen:

1. First, fire up Chrome, then click the three dots, and select Settings.

2. On the next screen, enter Payment in the search box, and press Enter.

3. It will list all it can find – one of these options will be Manage Payments; click it.

4. On the next screen, click Add; enter any fake credit card details you like, and hit Save.

5. You can now close the Settings window.

With a new payment method in place, we can now proceed with setting up a local version of our original demo.

Taking the Next Step

For our next demo, we're going to set up an instance of the Payment Request API to work locally, using the `local-web-server` package that is available to run under Node.js. Of course, if you have a preference for a different web server, then by all means use this – it must be set up with SSL support for our demo to work. Let's take a look and see what is involved.

MIGRATING TO LOCAL SETUP

For this demo, we'll assume that you use the hostname value of "localhost" – if you decide to use something different, then please adjust the steps accordingly. With this in mind, let's make a start:

1. We'll begin by extracting a copy of the `next step` folder from a copy of the code download that accompanies this book; save the folder to our project area that we created back in Chapter 2.

2. Next, go ahead and fire up your text editor, then open `payment.js` – we need to add in the script code that forms the basis of our checkout form. There is a fair bit to add, so we'll do it block by block, beginning with the `window.onload()` function to initiate our code:

```
window.onload = function(e) {

}
```

3. Next, we need to add in the function that take care of initiating the payment methods that we will support (and first saw in the CodePen version of this demo) – for this, go ahead and add in the following lines, immediately before the closing bracket of our `window.onload()` function:

```
const paymentMethods = [{
  supportedMethods: 'basic-card',
  data: {
    supportedNetworks: ['visa', 'mastercard', 'amex']
  }
}];
```

4. Immediately after the paymentMethods object, we now need to add in the various functions that will take care of displaying messages in our demo. We saw these back in the CodePen version, so let's add in the following after the closing double brackets of the paymentMethods const, leaving a line in between:

```
function displaySuccess() {
  document.getElementById("message").classList.add("success");
  document.getElementById("message").innerHTML = "<span>\u2714</span>
  Payment received - thanks for your order!";    }

function displayError() {
  document.getElementById("message").classList.add("failure");
  document.getElementById("message").innerHTML = "<span>\u2716</span>
  There was a problem with payment";
}

function displayMessage(mesg) {
  document.getElementById("message").classList.add("info");
  document.getElementById("message").innerHTML = "<span>&#128712;
  </span>" + mesg;
}
```

5. We now come to the core part of our code – the event handler that fires the Payment Request API, when we hit on our Buy Now button. First, leave a line after the previous function, then add in this:

```
document.querySelector(".pay-button").addEventListener("click",
function(e) {

})
```

6. Staying within the event handler block, we now need to add the meat of our demo – this is a substantial block, so we'll do this bit by bit. First up comes a declaration to clear any classes set against the message `<div>` element, which we need to add immediately after the opening line of the `pay-button` click event handler:

```
document.getElementById("message").className = ";
```

7. Next up comes the start of the `window.PaymentRequest` block – this starts by defining a number of variables, to handle calculations for shipping, tax, subtotal cost, and total values:

```
if (window.PaymentRequest) {
    let subtotal = Number(document.querySelector(".total-price").
    innerText);
    let shipping = 2.99;
    let tax = (subtotal + shipping) * 0.175;
    let total = Number(subtotal) + Number(tax) + Number(shipping);
```

8. We now need to add in the `paymentDetails` array object which takes care of defining the values we see in our checkout form:

```
const paymentDetails = {
  total: {
    label: 'Total due',
    amount: { currency: 'USD', value:  total.toFixed(2) }
  },
  displayItems: [{
    label: 'Coffee capsules',
    amount: { currency: 'USD', value: subtotal.toFixed(2) }
  },{
    label: 'Shipping',
```

```
      amount: { currency: 'USD', value: 2.99 }
   }, {
      label: 'Sales Tax',
      amount: { currency: 'USD', value: tax.toFixed(2) }
   }]
};
```

9. Now that our paymentDetails block has been defined, we can initialize
    it – we first need to set the paymentOptions variable, before calling the
    Payment Request API instance as request:

```
const paymentOptions = { requestPayerEmail: true };
let request = new PaymentRequest(paymentMethods, paymentDetails,
paymentOptions);
```

10. We're almost done – the contents of this final block is responsible for displaying
     the checkout form on screen and determining what action to take, based on
     what our customer selects:

```
if (request.canMakePayment) {
  request.canMakePayment().then(function(result) {
    if (result) {
      request.show().then(function(result) {
        result.complete('success').then(function() {
          console.log(JSON.stringify(result));
          displaySuccess();
        });
      }).catch(function(err) {
        if (err.message == "Request cancelled") {
          displayMessage("Request has been cancelled");
        } else {
          console.error(err.message);
          displayError();
        }
      });
    } else {
      console.log('Cannot make payment');
      displayMessage("Sorry - no valid payment methods available");
    }
```

```
    }).catch(function(err) {
      console.log(request, err);
    });
  }
}
```

11. At this point we now have all of our code in place, so go ahead and save this file as `payment.js` in the js subfolder under the folder you created back in step 1.

12. We can now preview the results of our work, so in order to do this, fire up a Node.js terminal session and change the working directory to the next step folder within our project area.

13. At the prompt, go ahead and enter this command:

```
ws –hostname localhost --https
```

It will look similar to the screenshot shown in Figure 3-1.

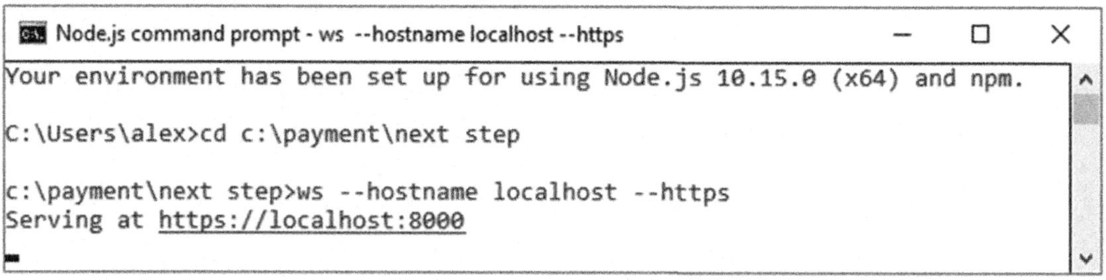

```
Node.js command prompt - ws --hostname localhost --https        —    □    ✕

Your environment has been set up for using Node.js 10.15.0 (x64) and npm.

C:\Users\alex>cd c:\payment\next step

c:\payment\next step>ws --hostname localhost --https
Serving at https://localhost:8000
```

Figure 3-1. *Sarting up our local web server*

14. Fire up Chrome (you will need to do this in Chrome; otherwise you will get SSL errors displayed). Now go ahead and browse to `https://locahost:8000/index.html` to preview the results of your work. If all is good, we should see something akin to the screenshot shown in Figure 3-2, once we've added at least one coffee capsule to our basket and clicked on Checkout securely.

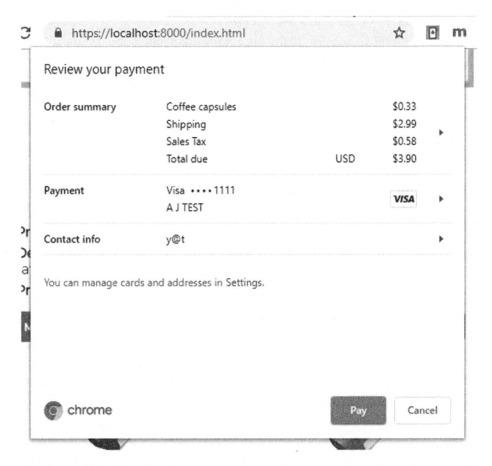

Figure 3-2. *Testing our local web server*

Although there were a fair few steps involved in setting up our demo, it was worth the effort to transition to a local setup – this gives us more flexibility in what we can do in terms of developing our final solution. There is a fair amount of code involved in this demo, so let's take a few minutes to work through it and understand how it all fits together.

Understanding How it Works

Assuming we've now had a moment to catch our breath, we should take a look at our code in more detail – it might seem a lot, but the key parts are all within the payment.js file, which includes code that we've already seen working in our previous CodePen demo.

We kick off this part of the demo with an event handler to load the API as soon as the window is ready – our first task is to define an array object `paymentMethods`, to store the various supported methods of payment.

Up next comes a set of functions to take care of the various messages that we display, such as for cancelled requests, a successful transaction (or heaven forbid) when our transaction results in a failure. We then initiate an event handler that fires up the API at the point of clicking our pay button.

Once inside the event handler, we first check to make sure that the browser supports the API (if not, it would fall back to a traditional checkout process, had we included one). If it is supported, we then define a number of variables to handle storage of values such as shipping, before defining the `paymentDetails` array object that is required for the API.

We then define a constant that covers the various options which require information from our customers (in this case, `requestPayerEmail`), before firing up the checkout form and directing the API to respond with the appropriate outcome based on the success or failure of our transaction. It finishes with displaying a message, if the API has been initiated, but is unable to proceed – this might happen if our customers have yet to embrace storing credit card details within the browser, for example!

Okay – let's move on: now that we have a demo set up to work locally, it's time we took things to the next stage and fine-tuned our example to turn it into a more complete solution.

Customizing the API Flow

A key point to remember is that the API itself is somewhat dumb: we can't use it to automatically work out discounts for example. At first, you might be forgiven for thinking that this means you can't implement features such as gift cards or discounts – this however is not the case!

The trick to this is remembering that as part of building up the configuration object that forms the API, we have to provide suitable labels and values, and that these need to be worked out *before we create our API object.* At the time of writing, it is likely you will need to specify these values within the same function; otherwise you may end up with instances where some values such as the initial "Goods" or "SubTotal" do not display correctly. As long as we create our API object correctly, then there are lots of opportunities available to hook in and provide extra features around the API.

Over the course of this chapter, we're going to explore some examples of how we might add in some of these features that you might typically see on an e-commerce web site, within the confines of the Payment Request API. There are effectively two types of changes we can make – those that relate to the form and those that relate to the payment process. Yes, it is true that they depend on each other: stay with me on this, and I will explain all!

Configuring Our Checkout Form

Okay – so what do I mean by two different types? Well, it is true that for a properly configured checkout, it's unlikely you can have some without others, but there is a difference between the two.

I mentioned that some fall into the group of form, and others relate to the payment process, right? Well, the key difference is *at what point* they are displayed in the overall process. The form ones are displayed at the point of clicking "Checkout" or "Buy Now" – but we have not launched the payment process by clicking that button.

The remainder falls into the group relating to the payment process: here we specify different requirements such as choosing a shipping method or asking the customer for a contact email address. Let's begin with taking a look at the form-based options in more detail first.

Setting a Display Icon

We're going to start with a really easy change, although there is a sting in the tail – I will come to that in a moment. For now, let us consider a typical favicon link we might use:

```
<link rel="icon" href="favicon.png" sizes="512x512" type="image/png">
```

Seems a sensible option to use, right? We can insert this within the <head> section of our markup – assuming the favicon is correctly located, you might assume this would display both in the browser tab and potentially in the checkout form, right?

Well – here's the sting in the tail: unfortunately, it does not yet appear anywhere in the checkout form! The only place we will see it is on the browser tab; the Payment Request working group have deemed this to not be part of the official specification for the API but as something best left for browser vendors to implement. At the time of writing, there doesn't appear to be any appetite for implementing this in browsers such as Chrome, but this might change in the future.

As a side note   If you're interested in seeing the comments about this, take a look at issue 707 on the W3C's GitHub issues log for the Payment Request API, at `https://github.com/w3c/payment-request/issues/707`.

Handling Different Currencies

Take another look at our code, and in particular the `paymentDetails` object – notice how we specify two values for each amount property? In each case we have to provide both the currency and value; in our demos thus far, we've specified USD or United States dollars as our currency. This clearly won't work for everyone – not everyone has a web site operating from the United States, and neither do we want to saddle our customers with extra costs such as credit card exchange fees!

Unfortunately, the API doesn't include support for automatically converting currencies for different countries; this is something we have to build into the shopping cart process prior to calling the API. Thankfully there is a trick we can use here, where instead of hard coding our currency value as indicated in this code extract:

```
const paymentDetails = {
  total: {
    label: 'Total due',
    amount: { currency: 'USD', value: total }
  },
```

...we can specify a variable placeholder to which we assign our unit of currency. It means that we can effectively work with lots of different currencies, including even Bitcoins! In reality though we may choose to support a select few; this might be based on where you have offices or what customers ask for as feedback.

A good reference for countries and their currency codes can be found at `www.currency-iso.org/dam/downloads/lists/list_one.xml`.

This is an easy change to implement, which will use the chilli demo we've already seen (but with slightly refactored code). Let's take a look and see what is involved to bring multicurrency support to our projects.

HANDLING MULTIPLE CURRENCIES

Before we get going on this demo, make sure you have saved a copy of the `currencies` folder from the code download that accompanies this book, to our projects area.

In preparation for the demo, I've refactored the HTML markup slightly, to make it easier to reference prices in code and to render currencies within their own elements and not as part of the same element as the prices or totals. I've also added in some markup – you can see it in the following and at line 10 in `index.html`:

```
<div id="currencies"><a id="usd" class="selected"><img src="images/
united-states.png">USD</a> | <a id="gbp"><img src="images/united-kingdom.
png">GBP</a></div>
```

With this in mind and once you've saved the folder, follow these steps:

1. We first need to add in two variables to cache these elements in code – for this, open payment.js then add in the following two lines of code on or around line 18, just after the `let subTotalText =....` declaration:

```
document.getElementById("gbp").classList.add("selected");
document.getElementById("usd").classList.remove("selected");
```

2. Next up, we need to add in two event handlers for our icons – these will take care of converting the prices from USD to GBP and vice versa:

```
gbp.addEventListener("click", function() {;
  console.log("GBP");
  document.getElementById("unitcost").innerText = 3.89;

  document.getElementById("gbp").classList.add("selected");
  document.getElementById("usd").classList.remove("selected");

  let els = document.querySelectorAll('.currency');
  els.forEach(function(el) {
    el.innerText = "£";
  });

  amount.click();
});
```

```
usd.addEventListener("click", function() {
  console.log("USD");
  document.getElementById("unitcost").innerText = 4.99;

  document.getElementById("gbp").classList.remove("selected");
  document.getElementById("usd").classList.add("selected");

  let els = document.querySelectorAll('.currency');
  els.forEach(function(el) {
    el.innerText = "$";
  });

  amount.click();
});
```

3. With event handlers in place, we now need to update the currencies displayed
    in our checkout form. For this, go ahead and add the following code,
    immediately before the `const paymentDetails = {` block, leaving a line
    blank between each block:

```
if (selected == "$") {
  currencyValue = "USD";
} else {
  currencyValue = "GBP";
}
```

4. We also need to add in two variables to help with taking care of switching
    currencies – go ahead and add in these two lines, immediately after the `let`
    `total =...` line. Make sure you leave a line blank after the second variable.

5. We now need to update our Payment Request API array object, so it recognizes
    which currency to display when the form is displayed. Go ahead and replace all
    instances of `'USD'` with `currencyValue`, so you end up with this:

```
const paymentDetails = {
  total: {
    label: 'Total due',
    amount: { currency: currencyValue, value: total }
  },
  displayItems: [{
    label: 'Sub-total',
```

```
      amount: { currency: currencyValue, value: subtotal }
  }, {
    label: 'Shipping',
      amount: { currency: currencyValue, value: 2.99 }
  }, {
    label: 'Sales Tax',
      amount: { currency: currencyValue, value: ax.toFixed(2) }
  }]
};
```

6. The last step is to add in some styling, to make our demo look presentable –
    add these at the end of the `styles.css` file in the currencies folder:

```css
/* currencies update */
#currencies {
  float: right;
  width: 150px;
  display: inline-block;
}

#gbp:hover, #usd:hover { cursor: pointer; }

#currencies > a { line-height: 24px; }

#currencies > a.selected {
  font-weight: bold;
  color: #8b0000;
}

#currencies > a:hover {
 color: #ff0000;
}

#currencies > a > img { width: 24px; height: auto; display:
inline-block; padding-right: 5px;  vertical-align: bottom; }
```

7. Finally, we can save our work and preview the results. Fire up a Node.js
    terminal window, then change the working folder to the `currencies` folder
    within our project area.

8. At the prompt, go ahead and enter this command:

    ```
    ws -hostname localhost --https
    ```

9. When Node confirms the web server is running, browse to `https://localhost:8000/index.html`; we will see the new flags in place (Figure 3-3).

Figure 3-3. *Our chillis demo with currency flags in place*

10. Click the GBP flag to display prices in pounds sterling, then add a few to the basket, and hit the Buy Chillis button. If all is well, we will see something akin to Figure 3-4, where we now display prices in pounds sterling, not US dollars.

Review your payment			
Order summary	Sub-total		£15.56
	Shipping		£2.99
	Sales Tax		£1.99
	Total due	GBP	£20.54

Figure 3-4. *Displaying prices in pounds sterling...*

Although our demo was somewhat simplistic in nature (after all, who would only sell one product, I wonder?), it serves to show the type of changes we need to allow the API to support multiple currencies. There are a few points we do need to consider though, so let's dive in and take a look at the code in more detail.

Exploring Our Code in More Detail

So – allowing for the fact that the API doesn't support conversion between currencies, how did we add in that support? Well, the trick here is to do the conversions *before* we feed the numbers into the API; as long as we don't include the currency denominators separately, the API doesn't really what the totals represent; they only make sense when we display the values on the form.

We kicked off by adding in a <div> element to host both the currency text labels and flag icons; the code was refactored before the start to ensure that the price and total values were displayed without the currency denominators in the same element (it makes it easier to switch out each value for its alternative). Once this was in place, we added two event handlers (usd.addEventListener and gbp.addEventListener) – these took care of updating the price displayed on screen, swapping over the currency units, and triggering an update on the total amount displayed on screen.

We then added a check to see what value was stored in currencyValue – this was switched between GBP and USD, depending on which flag was clicked. To be sure that the correct currency was displayed on the form, we also replaced all instances of 'USD' with currencyValue – this would then display the relevant currency on screen, as a three-letter code.

As an aside, it's worth noting that at the time of writing, we can't use commas as decimal separators within the API – doing so will generate an error similar to that in Figure 3-5.

```
❌ ▶ Uncaught TypeError: Failed to construct              pen.js:97
   'PaymentRequest': '19,95' is not a valid amount format for total
      at HTMLButtonElement.document.querySelector.onclick
   (pen.js:97)
```

Figure 3-5. *Trying to display values with comma separators...*

It does mean that for countries which use the comma as a decimal separator, we will have to revert to using standard decimal notation for the time being. The author has seen indications that it should be possible to display something using standard browser localization, but with an ever-changing API that is yet to be fully ratified as a standard, documentation on this subject is still somewhat scarce!

For more details on what is currently accepted in the standard, please refer to the W3C documentation, available at `www.w3.org/TR/payment-request/#validity-checkers`.

How Can We Handle Multiple Items Better?

By now, I'm sure you can't have failed to notice that our demos have been somewhat limited in terms of the number of items we're selling – there are very few outlets that will only sell one item!

The vast majority of shops will sell multiple items – hundreds, if not thousands: we're not going to go to that extreme though. Instead, we will expand the size of our demo shop to include a few more products; over the course of the next few pages, we'll use coffee pods as our example.

Now – you may be asking what this might have to do with the API, right? Well, there's a good reason for this: when it comes to initiating the checkout form, it has an effect on what we display in the form. Take a look at the screenshot shown in Figure 3-6 – at the moment, this displays all of the items we need to see, such as a subtotal, shipping, and sales tax.

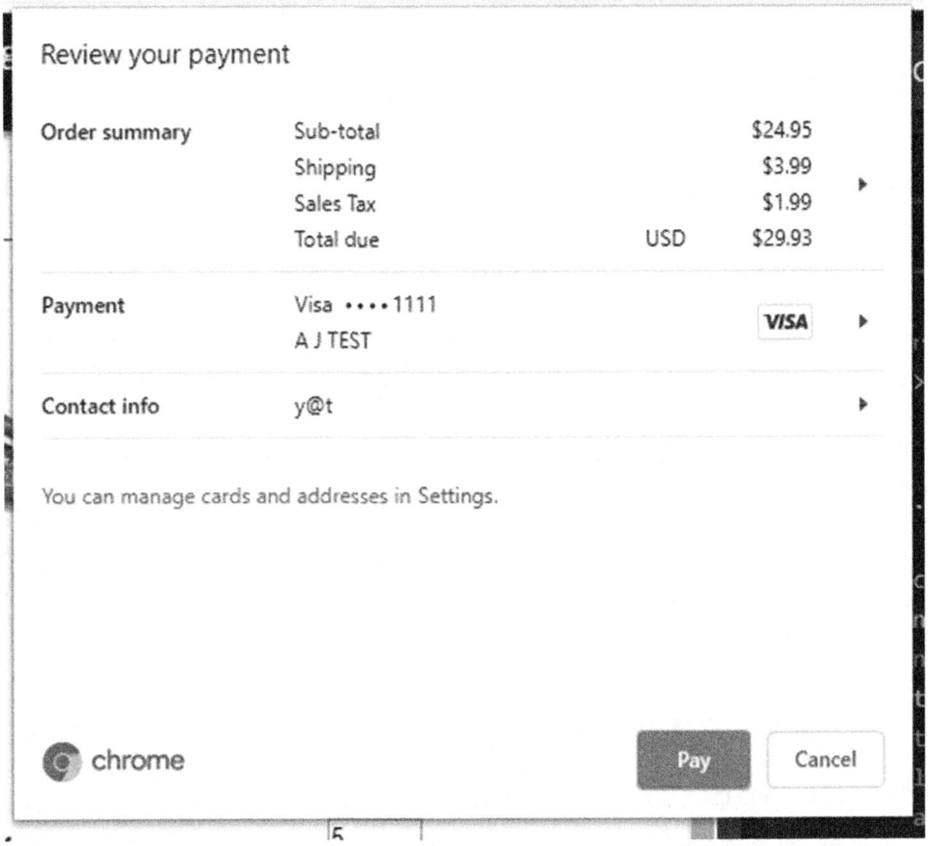

Review your payment

Order summary	Sub-total		$24.95
	Shipping		$3.99
	Sales Tax		$1.99
	Total due	USD	$29.93

| Payment | Visa ••••1111 | **VISA** ▸ |
| | A J TEST | |

| Contact info | y@t | ▸ |

You can manage cards and addresses in Settings.

○ chrome   [Pay]   [Cancel]

Figure 3-6. *A typical checkout form using the API*

If we start adding more products to our cart, we might want to display each – there is a limit though in terms of what we can display on the checkout form. Although we might want to display a list of all products at the time of sale, the API was never designed to display more than a top-level summary. It does not matter how many items we want to display – we are limited to only showing the first three plus the total.

We can display a longer list of items by clicking the arrow to the right of the order summary, but this comes at the expense of seeing an entry such as "plus 3 more items…" appear in the list. If we're not careful, this could result in us not displaying the key critical values at all or forcing customers to have to click through to the order summary page to see them.

What does this mean for us? Well, it does raise some important questions on what we can (or should) display – for example, we know that the overall total will always be shown, but what about subtotals, or entries such as discounts? There is one trick in our favor though: the order of items displayed on screen is controlled by the `displayItems[]` array in our code. To see what this means for us, let's dive into a quick walk-through that will work through how changing the order can affect what we see on screen and help us understand how best to display the relevant information effectively.

CHANGING THE ORDER

For this demo, we'll use a copy of the `change order` folder that is available in the code download; go ahead and save a copy of this folder to our project area, before following these steps:

1. First, fire up our local web server, then change the working directory to the change order folder, and browse to `https://localhost:8000/index.html`.

2. Click Add to Cart under the Fortissimo option, until you have at least 14 capsules added to cart.

3. Go ahead and click Checkout securely – you should see the details listed in Figure 3-7.

Review your payment			
Order summary	Coffee capsules		$2.76
	Shipping		$2.99
	2 more items		
	Total due	USD	$6.76

Figure 3-7. *Viewing the order of items*

At first glance, it seems straightforward enough, right? After all, our payment processor is really only interested in the final figure of $6.76; the form details what the customer has selected, plus the costs for the products and shipping.

This raises a couple of questions – what about tax (at least for those who need to know the figure)? The cost of the capsules isn't the original cost: this figure includes a $2 discount, but how does our customer know that this has been applied? The simple answer is that they can always click through to the details – this doesn't feel great though!

For argument's sake, if we had had clicked through, we would have seen the details listed in Figure 3-8.

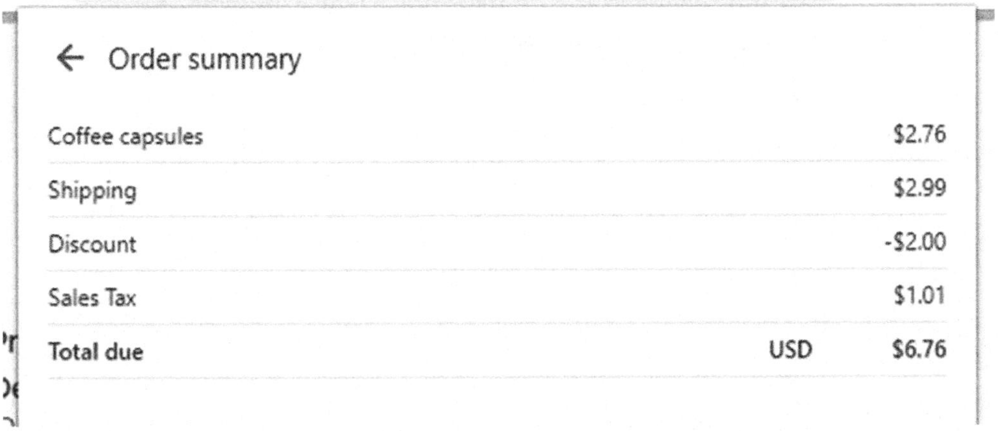

Figure 3-8. *Our form in more detail*

Granted, this will show the details our customer might need, but it means "one more click" is needed – can we do anything about this?

Well, in some respects we can: we might, for example, move the entries around:

4. Revert back to payment.js stored in the js subfolder, under the change order folder – look for this code:

```
,{
  label: 'Sales Tax',
  amount: { currency: 'USD', value: tax.toFixed(2) }
}
```

5. Move it up the block, so your code displays this:

```
displayItems: [{
  label: 'Coffee capsules',
  amount: { currency: 'USD', value: subtotal.toFixed(2) }
},{
    label: 'Sales Tax',
    amount: { currency: 'USD', value: tax.toFixed(2) }
  },{
  label: 'Shipping',
  amount: { currency: 'USD', value: 2.99 }
}, {
```

6. Save the file, then refresh the browser window, and re-add the same 14 capsules as we did earlier in the walk-through.

7. Click Checkout securely – if all is well, you will see the change effected in Figure 3-9.

Review your payment

Order summary	Coffee capsules		$2.76
	Sales Tax		$1.01
	2 more items		
	Total due	USD	$6.76
Payment	Visa ••••1111		VISA
	A J TEST		
Contact info	y@t		

Figure 3-9. *Our updated checkout form*

Here you will see the shipping entry has been replaced by the entry for sales tax – moving elements around in the request block will dictate which elements are displayed and in which order within the form.

Although this walk-through only required some simple changes, it has a profound effect on the overall experience for our customers – some customers may not care a lot about the details they see, while others want to see everything up front and will potentially abandon the cart if what they see affects their confidence level. This raises some important questions for us to consider, so let's pause for a moment to explore what this means in practice.

Exploring What this Means for Our Form

When using the API, we have to bear in mind that the summary was only designed to display three items – it will have an impact on what we display to our customers.

This means that we have to consider what information we display at this point – do we simply display the total cost and shipping and include extras such as discounts in the total cost figure? Our payment processor will only ever be interested in the final figure owed by the customer; we could potentially bundle everything into one entry which would be displayed alongside the total amount (the latter being a required field for the form).

Equally we may not really care about the order in which items are displayed – this might sound flippant, but we may take the view that as customers can see the total amount present, many will only be interested in this figure and skim over the rest. If this is the case, then we can choose which order items are presented and let the form handle how these are displayed in the summary and detail views.

Whichever route we decide to take, it's important to ensure that we make the labels sufficiently clear that we might be combining values (such as tax and shipping), or that in the case of discounts, we either display our subtotal and a separate entry for discounts or use a label that indicates the subtotal already includes the discounted amount. I suspect that customers may leave feedback to indicate what they would like to see, so it's worth bearing this in mind when choosing the overall order!

Accepting Gift Cards and Discounts

Ah yes – in this age of the Internet, it's a now de facto expectation that prices will be cheaper; if one has a discount or promotion code, then so much the better!

No matter what discounts or cards we offer, we still have to allow for them when working with the Payment Request API. The API doesn't include a dedicated feature to manage these as such; the only discounts (or charges) it can handle are related to payment by certain methods such as credit cards, which we'll cover later in this chapter.

However, this isn't an issue for us though: this type of discounting is something we would have to manage prior to initiating the Payment Request API. The key here is to remember that in terms of payment, we only need to provide limited details to our payment processor. We can work out and display the discount separately, as long as the final figure sent through reflects the discount, shipping, and taxes that the customer needs to pay.

This brings us nicely to our next demo – for our next exercise we're going to implement a basic 20% discount for every 10 coffee capsules a customer buys from our demo store. I know this may not represent reality (after all, 20% is a big discount!), but it's the concept behind it that counts: we're taking off the discount *before* we fire up the API and pass in the values to be displayed on our form. Let's take a look and see what's involved in more detail.

ACCEPTING DISCOUNTS

For this demo, make sure you've saved a copy of the `discounts` folder from the accompanying code download, into your project area. I've already added in some markup ready for this exercise – you can see it at or around line 12 in `index.html`:

```
<input id="amount" type="number" value="0" min="0">
    <div id="getmore">Add 2 more to get discount....</div>
```

Let's make a start with the following steps:

1. We first need to adjust our script – go ahead and open `payment.js` in your text editor.

2. Next, we need to declare a variable to store the amount of discount given. Add in this highlighted line, below the variable that caches the quantity shown in the amount input:

    ```
    let qty = parseFloat(document.getElementById("amount").value);
    let discountamt;
    ```

3. Next, we can now add in the calculations to determine if the discount message should be displayed, as well as work out what the discount amount should be. Add this in before the closing double bracket of the `amount.addEventListener` event handler:

```
// apply discount if over 10, or prompt if over 8
var disc = document.getElementById("amount").value;
if ((disc > 7)  && (disc < 10)) {
  document.getElementById("getmore").style.display="block";
} else if (disc == "10") {
  discountamt = Number(0.2 * subtotal);

  document.getElementById("getmore").innerText = "A 20% discount
  will be applied at checkout"
  document.getElementById("getmore").style.display="block";
} else {
  document.getElementById("getmore").style.display="none";
}
```

4. Although we have our event handler in place, it won't be any good if we're not passing through the right values to the API. For this we need to add in some additional calculations – look for this line (around line 54):

```
let qty = document.getElementById("amount").value;
```

...then add in the following below it:

```
if (discountamt == undefined) { discountamt = 0.00; }

let subtotal = Number(qty * 4.99);
let totaldisc = Number(subtotal - discountamt);
let shipping = 2.99;
let tax = (subtotal + shipping) * 0.175;
let total = Number(totaldisc) + Number(tax) + Number(shipping);
```

5. We have one more alteration to make – in the displayItems block (starting on or around line 70), add in this code as highlighted:

```
    amount: { currency: 'USD', value: subtotal.toFixed(2) }
}, {
  label: 'Discount',
  amount: { currency: 'USD', value: discountamt }
}, {
  label: 'Sub Total (after discount)',
```

6. Go ahead and save your work – we can now preview the results. Fire up a Node.js terminal window, then change the working folder to the `discounts` folder within our project area.

7. At the prompt, go ahead and enter this command:

    ```
    ws -hostname localhost --https
    ```

8. When Node confirms the web server is running, browse to `https://localhost:8000/index.html`; if all is well, we should see something akin to the screenshot, shown in Figure 3-10, once we've added ten bags to our basket.

Figure 3-10. *Applying a 20% discount...*

9. If we then begin the checkout process, we will see a discount has been applied (Figure 3-11) – to see proof that the prices have been adjusted, click the arrow to the right to display the full order.

← Order summary

Goods		$49.90
Discount		$9.98
Sub Total (after discount)		$39.92
Shipping		$2.99
Sales Tax		$9.26
Total due	USD	$52.17

Figure 3-11. *A 20% discount has been applied*

In the high pressure, high stakes world of retail, customers always expect some form of discount – if these are not offered, then you would need a pretty compelling offer to survive!

Over the course of this exercise, we've worked through implementing the basics of such a discount – granted, we might not want to offer quite as much in reality, but nevertheless the same principles still apply, no matter the size or specifics of the discount. Let's take a look at how we implemented this functionality in more detail.

Exploring Our Code in Detail

To set up a discount similar to the one we've developed required us to make changes in several places – we kicked off by adding in the basics of the banner in our markup, along with a message to encourage customers to buy more if they didn't have enough to qualify.

We then moved onto `payment.js` – we added a placeholder variable, `discountamt`, to store the amount of discount we will give; we then adjusted the amount event handler to determine if our placeholder message should be displayed or kept hidden. The next change was to put in a check to ensure that `discountamt` would be zero if the customer didn't qualify; otherwise we adjusted our shipping and tax calculations to ensure that the discount was applied at the right point. We finished off by amending the `paymentDetails` constant, to include an extra label to display if a discount had been applied, and the amount this equated to in dollars.

Thinking further afield, there are some important considerations we should bear in mind: what about security of discount codes? The API is pretty dumb, inasmuch as it doesn't contain support for validating such codes, so the responsibility falls to us developers to ensure this happens as expected.

Our demo was a simple affair to illustrate the principles of applying a discount and feeding that through to the API – you will notice that the more we play with it, the more we see some oddities in terms of what is (or is not) applied. For example, it hides the message if we add more than ten bags – clearly our demo would need further work before we could consider putting into production! The key lesson here is that not only is it important to ensure we pass the right values but that also our discount only kicks in at the right point and that we are clear with how it should be applied, particularly when using the API.

Configuring Our Payment Process

Okay – let's switch focus: so far, we've explored some of the changes we might implement to fine-tune the experience for our customers, before they hit our checkout form. However, this is just part of the process: what about once our checkout form is displayed?

In a similar vein, we can easily make changes to the payment process – for example, how about updating the "Buy Now" button to reflect that the browser is configured for the API and can allow a quick checkout? We've already touched on some of the options we can elect to use such as requesting email addresses – let's take a look at some of the other things we can add, beginning with validating the options we set around the information we ask for from customers.

Asking for Details from Customers

We've already touched on implementing this next tweak, but as it's an important one, it's worth covering again – configuring the details we ask for from our customers.

This might sound daft that we're trying to change something we've already covered, but it's important to understand that these options will not apply across the board to all projects. When considering requirements for each checkout form that we create, we should determine which values are required and which we can do without for that project.

In most cases, the information specified will ask customers for their name, phone number, and email address:

```
const options = {
  requestPayerName: true,
  requestPayerPhone: true,
  requestPayerEmail: true,
  requestShipping: true,
  shippingType: "delivery"
};
```

In each case, we will need to provide onchange-type handlers to allow for customers who change their selected option; we'll delve into this in more detail later in this chapter.

The odd-one out though is shipping – not only do we need to allow for customers to change their mind when selecting but also to ensure that our checkout form is updated to reflect any changes in prices or totals as a result of changing the selected shipping method. This is something we've already touched on in previous demos; we'll explore shipping as a subject in more detail in Chapter 4, but for now, let's have a quick look at how changing this option affects what is displayed in our checkout form.

ADDING THE REQUEST... OPTIONS

For this demo, we'll use a copy of the options folder that is available in the code download – save this at the root our project area, then follow these steps:

1. Go ahead and open payment.js within the options folder – look for this line on or around line 49:

   ```
   const paymentOptions = { requestPayerEmail: true};
   ```

2. Edit it as indicated – we'll add in the options we covered earlier in this section:

   ```
   const paymentOptions = {
     requestPayerName: true,
     requestPayerPhone: true,
     requestPayerEmail: true,
     requestShipping: true,
     shippingType: "delivery"
   };
   ```

3. Save the file – if we then preview our results in a browser, add a few packs of chillis to the basket, and click our Buy button, we'll see a typical checkout form appear. Take a closer look at this section – here, you may see some details, similar to those indicated in Figure 3-12.

Figure 3-12. *Displaying our updated options*

If it shows nothing, then:

4. Click the arrow to the right, and hit the Add Contact Info button to add in some details.

5. When you're done, hit Done, and navigate back to the Summary page.

Notice how we now see our chosen contact details present, alongside our name? At first glance this might look like we've added all of the available options; however, there is a problem.

The sharp-eyed among you should see that we've only included three options – what's happened to the shipping ones? By rights, there should be at least five label changes present, but we only have three! The reason for this is that the shipping options are the oddity among the pack; they need a little more configuring before we see the full benefit of what they can offer.

We'll complete the shipping options in more detail in the next chapter but suffice to know that we can enable the others as needed – their need will depend on what your site sells and whether it makes sense to have one of the options enabled for your site.

Adding Iframe Support

Our next change isn't an obvious one, unless you look at the markup we're about to use in more detail – the use of iframes.

There are some instances where we might need to use iframes to host our checkout form – a typical example might be when we're linking to a payment provider which requires their use, as part of any service provision or agreement. If we don't make any changes, then the checkout form will appear, but inside the iframe – clearly this won't work!

Thankfully there is a simple fix we can implement to get around this; as part of the iframe, we simply need to provide the `allowpaymentrequest` parameter when defining the iframe element:

```
<iframe src="URL_INCLUDING_PAYMENT_REQUEST_CALL" allowpaymentrequest></iframe>
```

Making this change will allow the checkout form to display correctly – our next exercise will show how easy it is to effect this change.

ADAPTING TO USE IFRAMES

Before we begin, make sure you have a copy of the iframe folder that is available in the code download that accompanies this book – save it as `iframe` in our project area, then follow these steps:

1. First, fire up your text editor, and add the following lines to a new file – these will serve as our host file for calling the API demo:

```
<!DOCTYPE html>
<html>
<head>
  <title>Viewing Payment Request API via an iframe</title>
  <link href="https://fonts.googleapis.com/css?family=Montserrat"
  rel="stylesheet">
</head>
<body>
  <h2>Viewing a Payment Request API via an iframe</h2>
  <iframe src="index.html"></iframe>
</body>
</html>
```

2. Save this as `iframe.html` at the root of the `iframe` subfolder.

3. If we were to run the demo now, it will run the product page, but the checkout cart will fail – for it to work, we need to add in this tag immediately after `"index.html"`:

```
allowpaymentrequest
```

4. To make our demo look a little more presentable, add the following style block immediately before the closing `</head>` tag in our code.

```
<style>
  body { font-family: 'Montserrat', sans-serif; }
  h2 { display: block; width: 565px; margin: 30px auto; }
  iframe { width: 570px; height: 1000px; margin: 20px auto 20px
  auto; border: none; display: block; }
</style>
```

5. Go ahead and save the file – we can now preview the results. Fire up a Node.js terminal window, then change the working folder to the `iframe` folder within our project area.

6. At the prompt, go ahead and enter this command:

    ```
    ws -hostname localhost --https
    ```

7. When Node confirms the web server is running, browse to `https://localhost:8000/iframe.html`. If all is working as expected, we will see our shop appear; the checkout form will appear correctly once we've clicked on a few products and hit the Checkout securely button.

A simple change, yet a critical one if we are forced to have to use iframes – the addition of one keyword is enough to allow the API to operate correctly in the browser, if the target page is being hosted in an iframe element elsewhere on the site. This would be the case if we decided to use the API but had to host it away from its host page for security reasons; making this change will allow the API to work as expected.

Handling Changes

Throughout the course of this chapter, we've worked through a number of options that we can add to fine-tune the experience for our customers. There is something missing though: what if customers want to change their mind about something they select?

This might be anything from changing email addresses, right through to changing shipping options. This might particularly be the case if they've chosen a paid for shipping option, and later realize that if they waited an extra day, they can get shipping for free!

Don't worry: we will cover this in more detail. Changes to details such as email address and phone number arguably fall under this category too, so we'll explore these and more in the next chapter, and changes to payment methods (including those that incur extra charges) in Chapter 5.

Handling Extra Information

Next time you purchase something online, take a careful look at the checkout process – have you ever needed to provide extra details to the retailer, to help with processing and delivering your order? This might be anything from a free text field to dedicated tick boxes with preset details. It doesn't matter how this is set up though; it's more important that we have some form of option to allow customers to pass on extra details if needed, and when it is made available in our code.

To see what I mean, the best way is to add something into one of our previous demos – that's a perfect excuse for another demo, methinks! Let's take a look at what is involved in more detail.

ADD IN DELIVERY INSTRUCTIONS

For this demo, take a copy of the next steps folder from the code download, and save it as extra info into your project area, then follow these steps:

1. First, go ahead and open index.html from within the folder, in your usual text editor.

2. We need to add in our free text area that will serve to capture any messages – for this, add the following code, as highlighted:

```
<div id="message"></div>
<div id="instructions">
  <h2>Add delivery instructions</h2>
  <p>Have any special requirements? You still have time to let us
  know:</p>
  <textarea id="additional-details-container"></textarea>
  <button id="delinstruct">Submit</button>
</div>
```

3. We now need to display this at the appropriate point – go ahead and add in this code, immediately after the call to the displaySuccess() function:

```
console.log(JSON.stringify(result));
displaySuccess();
const additionalDetailsContainer = document.getElementById
('instructions');
```

```
    additionalDetailsContainer.style.display = 'block';
    additionalDetailsContainer.focus();
  });
```

4. To finish it off, we just need to add some styling – add the following
    declarations at the bottom of the `styles.css` file in the `extra info` folder
    created at the start of this exercise:

```
#instructions { display: none; }
#instructions > h2 > span { float: left; }

textarea { width: 325px; height: 200px; }

#delinstruct { background-color: white; border: none; border-radius:
24px; cursor: pointer; font-size: 16px; padding: 16px 32px; width:
170px; background-color: #c21807; color: #ffffff;
  letter-spacing: 2px; font-weight: 700; margin: 20px 0 0 170px;
  display: block; margin-bottom: 20px; }

  #delinstruct:hover { background-color: #f31e09; }
```

5. Go ahead and save your work before previewing the results. Fire up a Node.js
    terminal window, then change the working folder to the `extra info` folder
    within our project area.

6. At the prompt, go ahead and enter this command:

```
ws -hostname localhost --https
```

7. When Node confirms the web server is running, browse to `https://
    localhost:8000/index.html`, then run through a test purchase, we should
    see a new text box appear at the end of the process (Figure 3-13, shown
    overleaf).

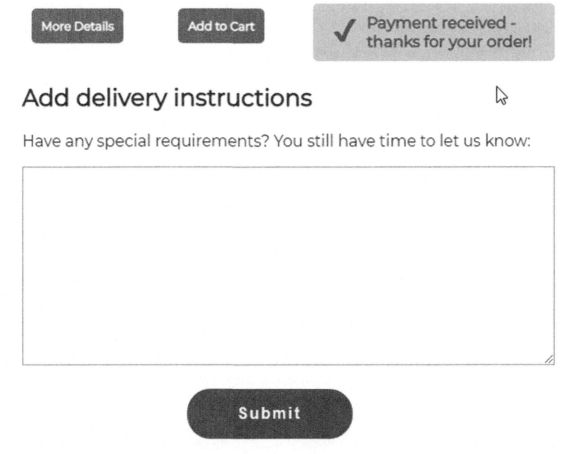

Figure 3-13. *Adding a box for delivery instructions*

This was a nice and easy change to make, yet one that will be a real boon to anyone who orders products and has…shall we say…a "less than standard address"? It's perfect for those who live in shared accommodation, where there might be an entry number to get into the building. There isn't a great deal involved in setting this up, but it's still worth taking a look in more detail.

Exploring the Code in Detail

A closer look at the code should indicate that there were minimal changes need to implement this option – we kicked off with adding in a `<textarea>` and button into our main markup. This works fine as they are both hidden initially; it saves us from hitting the DOM unnecessarily.

We then applied a change after calling `displaySuccess()`, to unhide the text area and set focus on it; this was finished off with some rudimentary styling to ensure it fitted in with the overall design of our test page.

Summary

When working with the Payment Request API, there are all manner of different ways to tweak the experience – some sit outside of the boundaries of the API, but many can directly affect the overall experience for our customer. Over the course of this chapter, we've covered a number of useful techniques to help sharpen that experience; let's take a moment to review what we've learnt.

We kicked off with setting up a version of the API to work locally – CodePen does work to an extent, but to get real flexibility, it's always better to be in control! We then moved onto starting to configure the checkout process – we started with a quick look at using favicons, although support for these is limited.

Next up, we covered handling different currencies, and how easy it is to alter the API to display the chosen currency. We then took a look at how best to display the relevant information (such as totals or discounts) the API, and we saw how changing the order has an effect on what is displayed in the checkout form.

We then took a look at how to accept discounts in the API – we focused on offering a discount for a select number of products, but this could easily be extended to work on promo codes, with the appropriate security. We then rounded out the chapter with a look at how we should choose what information to ask for from customers, along with giving them an opportunity to submit extra information to help with processing and delivery of their order.

By now, we've covered how to create and configure our checkout cart; it's time we shipped those products to our customers! There is a lot to cover on this; stay with me, and I will deliver all in the next chapter....

CHAPTER 4

Shipping

Picture the scene if you will – you've just been on a well-known web site, to order the latest tech; you've chosen free delivery because you're a cheapskate who won't pay shipping if you can at all help it.

The confirmation email says you'll get your delivery within 3-4 days, yet you then get an email a few hours later to say they've attempted delivery but failed...then you get another to say it's been delivered to your neighbor. A really confusing state of affairs – it looks like their systems just can't keep up...Contrast that with a UK online catalogue site that not only says it will deliver next day (and any day of the week at that), but will also deliver with a 2 hour window of your choice – yes, a 2 hour window.

See a picture here? Shipping is a key part of any e-commerce experience, yet is often wildly different between retailers, and not always lives up to expectations! Gone are the days of only delivering on a Monday to Friday; customers expect to be able to receive their goods any day of the week.

The one thing we as customers expect is a seamless process that makes it a snap to order products – granted, we can't control how well a third-party courier company performs but as developers can strive to provide the best online experience possible for our customers. The Payment Request API can absolutely help with this – we've covered the initial stages of setting it up and displaying prices; let's take a look at shipping works within the API, beginning with setting up a basic delivery option for customers.

Getting Started with Shipping

Cast your mind back to Chapter 2, when we first talked about setting up the `paymentOptions` constant – remember how we specified `requestPayerEmail` as the sole property in that constant?

© Alex Libby 2019
A. Libby, *Checking Out with the Payment Request API*, https://doi.org/10.1007/978-1-4842-5184-3_4

Well, it's time to revisit it and expand on this: the first part of setting up shipping within the API requires us to enable the option to request the shipping address, which we do using the `paymentOptions` object. We can then set up features to choose the delivery address and display a basic shipping option for our customers.

Don't worry though: it's really easy to do – the first task is to focus on getting the address, before we add in our supported shipping options. When setting up the address choices, we first add in the option to display any pre-saved addresses that are available to choose from, before dropping in an event handler that updates the selected address on screen. Let's take a look at how to set this up in more detail.

Obtaining the Shipping Address and Method

In this next exercise, we'll set up the option to request a delivery address, as well as include a basic shipping option; we will expand on the latter in a later exercise in this chapter. The first task is to enable the display (and selection) of a customer address, before we can then add in the various shipping options. At the end of this exercise, we will be able to run through a demo which allows us to select a customer address and have a default shipping set for us.

To set the address requires us to change the configuration object for the API and work `onShippingAddressChange` event handler – here's how we make use of it:

CHOOSING THE ADDRESS AND SETTING BASIC SHIPPING

For this first part of the demo, we'll be working with a copy of the `basic options` folder that is in the code download which comes with this book. Make sure you have a copy of this folder saved to our project area, before continuing with these steps:

1. We'll start by opening up a copy of the payment.js file from within the customer address folder – look for this code, on or around lines 45-46:

    ```
    amount: { currency: 'USD', value: tax.toFixed(2) }
    }]
    ```

2. Add a comma immediately after the closing brackets, then drop in this code:

```
}], shippingOptions: [{
        id: 'freeShippingOption',
        label: 'Free worldwide shipping',
        amount: {
        currency: 'USD',
        value: '0.00'
    },
    selected: true
    }]
};
```

3. To activate it, we need to set our Payment Request API object to ask for a shipping address – go ahead and amend this line as indicated:

```
const paymentOptions = { requestPayerEmail: true, requestShipping: true };
```

4. Next up, we can now add in the event handler to deal with updating the display if the customer decides to use a different address. As a start, look for this line:

```
let request = new PaymentRequest...
```

5. Leave a blank line, then add in this function:

```
request.addEventListener('shippingaddresschange', function(e) {
  e.updateWith(new Promise(function(resolve) {
    // No changes in price based on shipping address change.
    resolve(paymentDetails);
  }));
});
```

6. Go ahead and save the file. We can now preview the results of our work, so in order to do this, fire up a Node.js terminal session and change the working directory to the `basic options` folder within our project area.

7. At the prompt, go ahead and enter this command:

```
ws -hostname localhost --https
```

8. Fire up Chrome (you will need to do this in Chrome; otherwise you will get SSL errors displayed). Now go ahead and browse to `https://localhost:8000/index.html`, then if we select a few products to add into the basket, and click Checkout securely, we should see the option to choose a delivery address and shipping method appear (as indicated in Figure 4-1).

Delivery address	J Smith	
	Mr, Any Company, Po Box 10372, 124 Anywhere Stree...	▶
	+44 1234 567890	
Delivery method	Free worldwide shipping	
	$0.00	▶

Figure 4-1. *The initial delivery address and shipping options displayed*

9. Try clicking the arrow to the right and selecting any address you have already set up – clicking it will select that address, which is then displayed in our checkout form, such as the example in Figure 4-2.

Delivery address	Nicky Amato	
	2691 Honey Grove Forest, Cleveland Corners, Vermon...	▶
	+1 802-605-3618	

Figure 4-2. *The updated delivery address option*

For now, it's worth noting that you won't be able to change the shipping option, as we only have one set – this will change in a later exercise.

Although this was a simple change to effect, it is nevertheless a key one – most of the shipping options we will work with in this chapter require us to have an address of some description set in our form. With an address in place, this will open up a few options to us – there are some important points to be aware of, so let's explore how this code works in detail.

Exploring How this Works in Detail

When working with the shipping part of the Payment Request API, it's important to bear in mind that there are no clear-cut dividing lines in terms of what we can add as code.

The original intention of this exercise was to focus on just adding the address; it soon became clear that for it to work as expected, we would also have to add in at least one shipping option! In a way this makes sense, as we wouldn't be able to fulfill our delivery promise without both bits of information. Indeed, if we had not specified a shipping option too, it would result in the error shown in Figure 4-3.

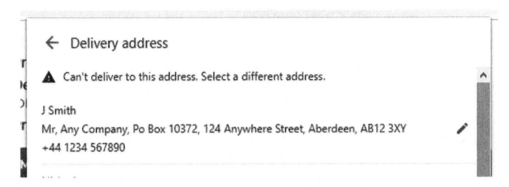

Figure 4-3. *Choosing an address with no suitable shipping option set*

To avoid this, we have to specify not only the `shippingaddresschange` event handler (in this case, on line 49) – which in itself uses a `Promise` to set and resolve (or fulfill) changes to selected addresses against our `paymentDetails` array object. We also have to add in the `shippingOptions` property to our `paymentDetails` constant, in order for us to be able to display and select a new address.

This means that if we're planning to use the API, making this change is something we would need to factor into our planning, so that when it comes to testing the change of address, it will select the new address without throwing an error!

Once we've set this up, there are a number of properties we can access directly – these are stored in the `PaymentAddress` interface. They relate to the various elements that make up a standard postal address, such as recipient, postal code, or city. Most values are returned in string format, except for `addressLine` – we can easily test how this works by adding in one line of code to our event handler, as shown:

```
      resolve(paymentDetails);
      console.log(request.shippingAddress);
  }));
```

In this case, the response returned will show the full (selected) shipping address of the customer from our API object, as indicated in Figure 4-4.

```
▼ PaymentAddress 🔲
  ▶ addressLine: ["2691 Honey Grove Forest"]
    city: "Cleveland Corners"
    country: "US"
    dependentLocality: ""
    languageCode: "en"
    organization: ""
    phone: "+18026053618"
    postalCode: "05078-7590"
    recipient: "Nicky Amato"
    region: "VT"
    sortingCode: ""
  ▶ __proto__: PaymentAddress
```

Figure 4-4. The response from request.shippingAddress

A full list is available in the cheat sheet PDF that is in the code download which accompanies this book, or you can see the latest version at `https://developer.mozilla.org/en-US/docs/Web/API/PaymentAddress`.

Okay – let's move on: now that we can choose a delivery address and use the provided shipping method, it's time to expand the number of shipping options available to us, to reflect what we are likely to have in a real-world scenario.

Yes, it is true that some companies may offer just free worldwide shipping, but not everyone will: it's more likely we would see several options available. Let's take a look to see what changes we need to make to include these extra shipping options in more detail.

Making Use of Details in Payment Request API

Before we start to expand on our shipping options, there is one useful little feature that is worth exploring – if you tried the tip toward the end of the last exercise explanation, you will have seen a JSON-formatted response be returned from the API, right?

Although it is useful to have this to confirm what has been submitted during testing, there may be occasions where you might want to use elements from this data elsewhere. To do this, we can make use of the toJSON method that comes with the API – adding it in would look something like this:

```
request.addEventListener('shippingaddresschange', function(e) {
    ....
    console.log(request.shippingAddress.toJSON());
  }));
});
```

When run, we will see output similar to that displayed in Figure 4-5.

```
{"requestId":"939e373f-d352-462f-b65c-d45be0a5d2f9","methodName":"basic-      payment.js:102
card","details":{"billingAddress":{"addressLine":["Any Company, Po Box 10372, 124 Anywhere
Street"],"city":"Aberdeen","country":"GB","dependentLocality":"","organization":"Mr","phone
":"+441234567890","postalCode":"AB12 3XY","recipient":"J
Smith","region":"","sortingCode":""},"cardNumber":"4111111111111111","cardSecurityCode":"22
2","cardholderName":"A J TEST","expiryMonth":"04","expiryYear":"2022"},"shippingAddress":
{"country":"GB","addressLine":["Any Company, Po Box 10372, 124 Anywhere
Street"],"region":"","city":"Aberdeen","dependentLocality":"","postalCode":"AB12
3XY","sortingCode":"","organization":"Mr","recipient":"J
Smith","phone":"+441234567890"},"shippingOption":"standard","payerName":null,"payerEmail":"
y@t","payerPhone":null}
> |
```

Figure 4-5. *This output from using the .toJSON method*

We can take it one step further and reference specific piece of information – for example, if we entered this command in the shippingaddresschange event handler:

```
console.log("Country: " + request.shippingAddress.country);
```

...we will get just the country of the selected shipping address displayed in console, as indicated in Figure 4-6.

```
Country: US
> |
```

Figure 4-6. *Displaying a specific value from shippingAddress*

It's a small but very useful feature – we will make use of this more, when we explore adding in delivery restrictions later in this chapter.

Expanding Our Shipping Options

In the previous exercise, we covered how to add in an option to display (and choose) a customer's address, as well as having to provide a basic shipping option to allow us to change the address as expected. I suspect many companies may not want to offer free worldwide shipping, as it will soon many players out of business very quickly!

Thankfully this is easy enough to rectify – we can add in more realistic shipping options, by making changes to two arrays – `shippingOptions` and `displayItems`. The former is required to display a shipping item in the checkout form, while the latter contains the options that we will use to update what is displayed on the form. Let's dive in and explore this in more detail.

EXPAND OUR SHIPPING OPTIONS

For the purposes of this exercise, we will use a copy of the completed `basic options` folder – make sure you save it as `expand options`, before continuing with these steps:

1. We'll begin by opening a copy of the `payment.js` file from within the expand options folder, in your usual text editor – look for this line of code, on or around line 39:

```
amount: { currency: 'USD', value: subtotal.toFixed(2) }
```

2. Immediately below it, you will see the "Free worldwide shipping" option; alter it as highlighted:

```
}, {
  label: 'FREE delivery (3-5 days)',
  amount: { currency: 'USD', value: shipping.toFixed(2) }
}, {
```

3. Next, we now need to add in our updated shipping options – for this, look for the `shippingOptions` array, which starts on or around line 46. Go ahead and remove lines 47-53, then add in the new choices as indicated:

```
}], shippingOptions: [{
        id: 'standard',
        label: 'FREE delivery (3-5 days)',
        amount: {currency: 'USD', value: '0.00'},
```

```
            selected: true,
          },
          {
            id: 'express',
            label: 'Express delivery (next day)',
            amount: {currency: 'USD', value: '3.99'},
          },
        ],
      };
```

4. We're done with making changes – go ahead and save the payment.js file. We can now preview the results of our work, so in order to do this, fire up a Node.js terminal session and change the working directory to the expand options folder within our project area.

5. At the prompt, go ahead and enter this command:

```
ws –hostname localhost --https
```

6. If we browse to https://localhost:8000/index.html to preview the results, then add in some products to our basket, and hit Checkout securely, we will see our updated default shipping option (Figure 4-7).

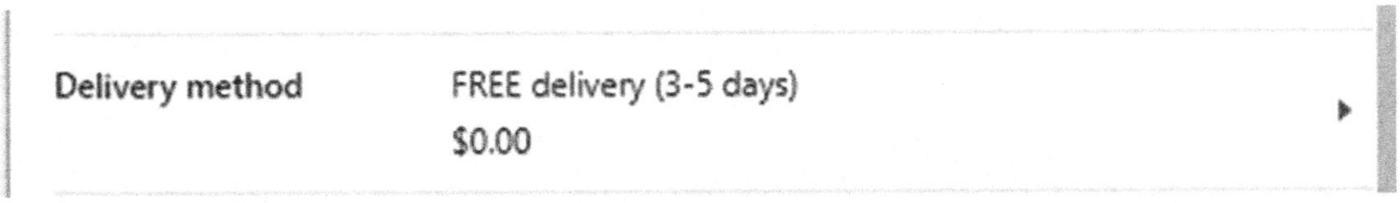

| Delivery method | FREE delivery (3-5 days) | ▶ |
| | $0.00 | |

Figure 4-7. *Our updated default shipping option*

If we were to click the right arrow to try to change the option, it will indeed present the alternatives and allow you to click them. However, if you do so, it won't update the selection shown on screen – instead, we will be presented with the error shown in Figure 4-8, if we were to look in console.

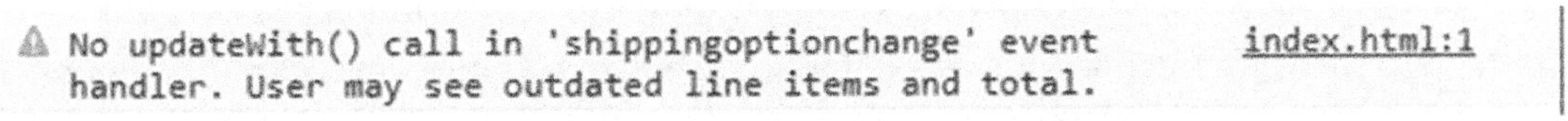

```
⚠ No updateWith() call in 'shippingoptionchange' event        index.html:1
  handler. User may see outdated line items and total.
```

Figure 4-8. *The error when shippingoptionchange event is not present*

Don't worry, this is expected – it's something we need to bear in mind when planning changes as part of implementing the API. The fix for this will be to add in an event handler – we will do this in a new exercise shortly, but for now, let's review the changes we've made to our demo in more detail.

Exploring the Changes Made

The changes we've made in this exercise are probably some of the easiest we need to make – a part of the structure is already in place, from when we initially specified just one option for shipping.

In this exercise, the only changes we needed to make were to update the default text displayed in `displayItems` and add in new options under the `shippingOptions` array. There is however one small point to make – in the shippingOptions array, we need to specify the selected property against one of the shipping options. This is the one that will be shown as ticked if we select to change them, as shown in Figure 4-9.

Figure 4-9. *Choosing from the available delivery options*

This becomes more important when we look at updating the chosen option in the next exercise; if we don't, then the selected option will remain unchanged, but that we won't see any errors appear in console either!

Okay – let's move on: we now have our expanded shipping options in place, but for them to work, we need to alter our demo to reflect any changes made by customers when choosing an appropriate shipping option during purchase. There are a couple slightly more involved changes to make to achieve this, so let's explore what's required in more detail.

Dealing with Changes to Shipping

At the end of the last exercise, we ended up with an updated checkout form that now has a couple of delivery methods set – trouble is, we can try selecting the one not set as much as we like, but it will not update our form! The reason for this is that we're missing code: the `shippingoptionchange` event handler is used to determine if a new delivery choice has been made and update the checkout form accordingly.

This method works in a similar way as the `shippingaddresschange` method we saw at the beginning of this chapter – both have a similar name, and both initiate a new Promise that is fulfilled once our customer has selected the appropriate option.

However, there is one key difference – with the `shingaddresschange` event handler where we simply select an address; with `shippingoptionchange` we not only need to select a delivery method but also need to update the final total to reflect any changes in shipping costs. Fortunately, this is easy enough to do, so let's dive into our next exercise and see what needs to happen in more detail.

DEALING WITH SHIPPING CHANGES

For this demo, we'll be using a copy of the expand options folder and building on where we left off from the previous exercise. Save a copy of the updated folder from the previous exercise as update shipping, then continue with the following steps:

1. We'll start by opening up a copy of payment.js from the new folder, into text editor. Once open, leave a blank line, then add in this code immediately after the displayMessage() function:

```
function updateDetails(details, shippingOption, resolve, reject,
stotal) {
  if (shippingOption === 'standard') {
    selectedOption = details.shippingOptions[0];
    otherOption = details.shippingOptions[1];
    details.total.amount.value = stotal;
  } else if (shippingOption === 'express') {
    selectedOption = details.shippingOptions[1];
    otherOption = details.shippingOptions[0];
    details.total.amount.value = (Number(stotal) + Number(3.99)).
    toFixed(2);
```

```
    } else {
      reject('Unknown shipping option: \" + shippingOption + '\");
      return;
    }
    selectedOption.selected = true;
    otherOption.selected = false;
    details.displayItems.splice(2, 1, selectedOption);
    resolve(details);
  }
```

2. Next, scroll down to the closing brackets at line 88, then leave a line and add in this event handler, to take care of updating our chosen shipping option:

```
request.addEventListener('shippingoptionchange', function(evt) {
  evt.updateWith(new Promise(function(resolve, reject) {
    updateDetails(paymentDetails, request.shippingOption, resolve,
    reject, total);
  }));
});
```

3. That's all the changes we need to make – at this point, save the file and close it. We can now preview the results of our work, so in order to do this, fire up a Node.js terminal session and change the working directory to the next step folder within our project area.

4. At the prompt, go ahead and enter this command:

```
ws -hostname localhost --https
```

5. We can now preview the results of our changes – if we browse to `https://localhost/index.html` in a browser, then add in some products to the basket and hit Checkout securely, we will see our now familiar checkout form.

6. Try clicking the arrow to the right of Delivery method, then select the Express delivery option – if all is well, we will now see this appear under Delivery method, as shown in Figure 4-10.

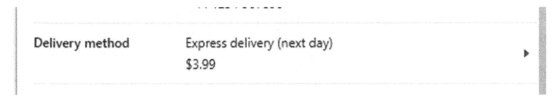

Figure 4-10. *Displaying the updated shipping method*

This was a quick and easy change to make but one that means our shipping options resemble something closer to a real-life example! The code we've implemented shows off usage of a couple of key points we should cover, so let's take a moment to explore them in greater detail.

Breaking Apart Our Code

If we had to pick a single change which was more complex than the others in this chapter, then this would probably rank in the top few – even though it isn't as complicated as it might first seem!

At the heart of this exercise lies the updateDetails function – into this we pass details of the paymentDetails array object (that stores all of the labels and values you see on the form), alongside the chosen shipping option and a Promise for this action. We then do a check of each shipping type (by ID), to determine which was selected before we apply the changes. In each case we use selectedOption to store the chosen value, the otherOption variable to store the option we didn't select, and the paymentDetails value is updated.

The important part is that once updated, we then have to state which shipping option should be marked as selected (selectedOption.selected = true;), before splicing in the updated total value as appropriate. These details are then used to update the paymentDetails array object, before marking our Promise as complete.

Implementing Delivery Restrictions

Up until now, the shipping options we've implemented will suit some retailers, but not all – many retailers will need to implement certain restrictions on what can be delivered and where that package can be sent. A typical example might be if they can't guarantee safe delivery of a product to some countries, or potentially there may be export restrictions on certain products. If this is the case, then how might we implement something using the Request Payment API?

Although the API doesn't contain built-in functions to control where deliveries can be made, we can nevertheless still implement something relatively easily. I say relatively easily, as the concept is technically very straightforward; what might make things more complicated are the conditions behind the restrictions! One of the simpler ways to restrict deliveries is purely by region or country. For example, we can build conditions that limit free delivery to the retailer's home state, while those who are out of state will have to pay postage. Let's dive in to our next exercise, to see how we might implement such conditions when it comes to determining delivery options in the API.

IMPLEMENTING SHIPPING RESTRICTIONS

Before we get started on setting up our demo, we will need to take a copy of the `update shipping` folder from the previous exercise and save it as `restrictions` at the root of our project folder. Once done, go ahead with these steps:

1. As per before, we first need to open up a copy of `payment.js` from the update shipping folder, into our text editor – go ahead and modify the `displayMessage()` function. It's a little complex, so we'll break down into sections, beginning with setting an array object to store our base shipping option:

```
function updateDetails(details, shippingAddress, callback, stotal) {
  let shippingOption = {
    id: ",
    label: ",
    amount: {currency: 'USD', value: '0.00'},
    selected: true,
    pending: false,
  };
```

2. Immediately after it, add in the first part of this condition check – this determines if we're shipping to an address in California, USA, or to another States-based address:

```
if (shippingAddress.country === 'US') {
  if (shippingAddress.region === 'CA') {
    shippingOption.id = 'californiaFreeShipping';
    shippingOption.label = 'Free shipping in California';
```

```
    details.total.amount.value = Number(stotal).toFixed(2);
  } else {
    shippingOption.id = 'unitedStatesStandardShipping';
    shippingOption.label = 'Standard shipping in US';
    shippingOption.amount.value = '3.99';
    details.total.amount.value = (Number(stotal) + Number(3.99)).
    toFixed(2);
  }
  details.shippingOptions = [shippingOption];
  delete details.error;
} else {
```

3. The last part of this function takes care of flagging an error message if the address is not based in the United States:

```
  // Don't ship outside of US for the purposes of this example.
  shippingOption.label = 'Shipping';
  shippingOption.pending = true;
  details.total.amount.value = '55.00';
  details.error = 'Cannot ship outside of US.';
  delete details.shippingOptions;
}
details.displayItems.splice(1, 1, shippingOption);
callback(details);
}
```

4. Next, go ahead and remove the `shippingoptionschange()` event handler – this is no longer needed, as the equivalent is built into the `shippingaddresschange()` handler.

5. Now, look for the `shippingaddresschange()` method on or around line 98 – go ahead and replace it with this function:

```
request.addEventListener('shippingaddresschange', function(evt) {
  evt.updateWith(new Promise(function(resolve) {
    updateDetails(paymentDetails, request.shippingAddress, resolve);
  }));
});
```

6. With the changes made, go ahead and save your work.

7.   We can now preview the results of our work, so in order to do this, fire up a Node.js terminal session and change the working directory to the next step folder within our project area.

8.   At the prompt, go ahead and enter this command:

```
ws -hostname localhost --https
```

9.   We can now preview the results in a browser. Browse to `https://localhost:8000/index.html`, then add some products into the basket, and click Checkout securely. When we see the checkout form, notice how the delivery method section is not present, as shown in Figure 4-11.

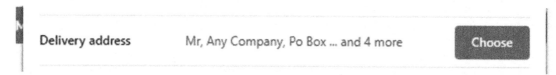

| Delivery address | Mr, Any Company, Po Box ... and 4 more | Choose |

Figure 4-11. *The new delivery address section*

10. If we click the arrow to the right, and choose a pre-saved address, we might see one of two things happen. If it is a US-based address, then our checkout form will display the updated address (Figure 4-12).

| Delivery address | Nicky Amato
2691 Honey Grove Forest, Cleveland Corners, Vermon...
+1 802-605-3618 | ▶ |
| Delivery method | Standard shipping in US
$5.00 | ▶ |

Figure 4-12. *Displaying a valid address...*

11. If we click an address that happens to be invalid (in this case, not based in the United States), then we will see the error shown in Figure 4-13, appear.

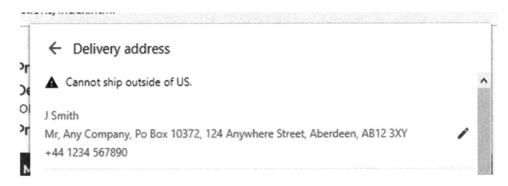

Figure 4-13. *...or prevented from choosing an invalid address*

This last exercise opens up some real possibilities for us, in terms of developing any checkout that uses the API – we can decide to limit deliveries to particular countries, force others to have to pay for postage, or even block delivery of certain products to customers!

Even though the conditions behind this feature could potentially become very complex, the basic principle will still be the same – establishing the condition, verifying if we've met it, and updating the available delivery options as appropriate. The code we've developed covers some important points that we should consider when developing checkout forms, so let's take a closer look at that code again, in more detail.

Breaking Apart the Code

In this latest demo, we take a whole new approach to how we select both the address and shipping methods – before, we've used a `shippingaddresschange()` method to trigger the former, with a separate option to manage the selection of our chosen shipping method. In the case of the restrictions demo, we've done away with the latter and rely solely on the former to manage changes of both the address and shipping options.

How does this work? Well, it's based on the principle of determining where we send the package to first, and that this directly influences *how* we send the package. The key difference in code this time is that whereas we weren't changing the address before (so could resolve it immediately), this time we pass in a different set of parameters (such as `paymentDetails`), and can only resolve it once we've updated them.

The update process is taken care of by the `updateDetails` function – inside this, we create a placeholder `shippingOption` array object, which is then updated based on (a) which country is referenced in the address, and (b) is it based in California. If the answer to either (or both) is yes, we then set the shipping.id value to the chosen option, alongside the appropriate `shippingOption`. label to use and update the total. Assuming this was successfully updated, we then update the current `paymentDetails` object with the new shipping details before deleting the error placeholder.

If it isn't successful (i.e. the customer trying to ship to a forbidden location), then we still update the details but this time set `shippingOption.pending` to true. This indicates we are still in the process of updating the delivery address; we also display a suitable error message on screen using the `details.error` property. We then finish by splicing in the new values to the displayItems configuration object, before firing the callback to update the paymentDetails object in our code.

Okay – time to change tack: our examples thus far haven't really touched much on how we might deal with any errors in the API. If we've built and tested our solution fully (as I am sure we would all do!), then we should be able to keep errors to a minimum. However, it's likely that customers will still come up with something that causes an issue, so let's pause for a moment to consider what errors we might need to handle in our projects.

Dealing with Errors

As a developer, I'm sure you'll agree that no solution will ever be 100% bulletproof and that we will always have something to fix, right? In an ideal world, customers would use what we design as we intended – trouble is, customers are fickle creatures at the best of times, and someone will try to do something that we did not intend should happen!

Although the Request Payment API is still something of a work in progress, it has nevertheless become pretty stable; there are however places where it might trip us up if we're not careful and don't make suitable allowances in our code.

The type of errors we can encounter can fall into one of two camps, those seen by the customer and those that we might generate during development or testing. Let's take a look at both in turn, starting with those seen by the customer.

Customer-Generated Errors

This group of errors is likely to appear as a result of resolving the Promise that is generated when initiating an instance of the Payment Request API; these range from simply aborting the transaction through to security issues that appear during a purchase. The supported errors that are returned are listed in Table 4-1.

Table 4-1. *Errors generated from the initiated Promise*

Error message	Purpose
AbortError	The returned promise rejects with an AbortError if the user agent is already showing a payment panel. Only one payment panel may be visible at a time across all documents loaded by the user agent. The promise is also rejected with AbortError if the user cancels the payment request.
InvalidStateError	The promise rejects with an InvalidStateError if the same payment has already been shown for this request (its state is interactive because it is being shown already).
NotSupportedError	The promise rejects with a NotSupportedError if the user agent does not support the payment methods specified when the PaymentRequest constructor was called.
SecurityError	The promise rejects with a SecurityError if the call to show() was not in response to a user action, such as a click or keyup event. This error can also be thrown at the discretion of the browser, if, for example, show() is being called while payment requests are blocked by parental controls.

Source: MDN

There is an important point to note here – if such an error is generated, then the customer would reasonably expect to want to try again, which might present a problem for us.

Why? Well, the good news is that the API does have a method that we can use – paymentResponse.retry() was designed for this purpose. The trouble is, not every browser supports it yet – at the time of writing, Chrome and Firefox both support it, but Edge and Opera have yet to implement it in their browsers. It does mean that if we want to make use of it, we will have to manually set up a get-out, so that we can at least allow customers to retry. The downside is that they may have to start from the beginning again, but this is a temporary workaround until browsers fully support the retry() method.

Errors Generated During Development

From a developer perspective, there are more places where our projects might trip up if we omit to include certain properties or do not define them correctly. A typical point of failure is if we don't specify a total value (which is obligatory) or if we miss out any of the labels you've seen in the exercises, from within the displayItems array. Let's look at some of the example errors we might see during development, which are listed in Table 4-2.

Table 4-2. *Types of development errors*

Issue	Error shown in console
No total value present	TypeError: Failed to construct 'PaymentRequest': Must specify total
Missing label, amount, currency, or value properties in displayItems[]	Failed to construct 'PaymentRequest': required member XXXXX is undefined. – where XXXXX might be amount, currency, value, or label; it does **not** specify where the error is in the code.
Negative values for total	'PaymentRequest': Total amount value should be non-negative
Invalid currency format	'PaymentRequest': '...' is not a valid ISO 4217 currency code, should be 3 upper case letters [A-Z]
Creating a long Promise that doesn't resolve in a timely manner	DOMException: Timed out as the page didn't resolve the promise from change event Note – this can also appear if we don't call event.updateWith() in our code.
Missing options in the shippingOptions array	DOMException: required member XXXXX is undefined. where XXXXX might be id, label, amount, currency or value; it does **not** specify where the error is in the code.

In addition, although it doesn't generate an error in the strictest sense, we must be careful to mark at least one option with the selected property. If we don't, then we run the risk of putting our customers into an endless loop which puts them back to the start, ready to select a shipping method again. If we however do the opposite (and set multiple entries with the selected property to true), then the last entry marked will be the one displayed with the tick on screen.

Okay – enough chitchat: it's time we saw some action! Some of the errors we've just talked about don't just affect shipping; they can crop up at any point in our development. However, there are four errors that will crop up when configuring the shipping part of our form – all of them are easy to fix: let's take a look at them in more detail, as part of the next exercise.

DEALING WITH ERRORS

For the purposes of this next demo, we will use a copy of the `update shipping` demo from earlier – save it as `spot errors` at the root of our project area, before continuing with these steps:

1. The first error we will deal with is one of duplicate IDs – go ahead and open up a copy of the `payment.js` file from the spot errors folder, into your text editor.

2. Next, look for this line in the code, on or around line 76:

   ```
   id: 'express',
   ```

3. Change it to `id: 'standard';` and save the file.

4. We can now preview the results of our work, so in order to do this, fire up a Node.js terminal session and change the working directory to the `spot errors` folder within our project area.

5. At the prompt, go ahead and enter this command:

   ```
   ws -hostname localhost --https
   ```

6. If we browse to `https://localhost:8000/index.html` to preview the results, then add in some products to our basket, and hit Checkout securely.

What happens? We will find that the checkout form doesn't appear – instead, we will get the error shown in Figure 4-14 appear in the browser console.

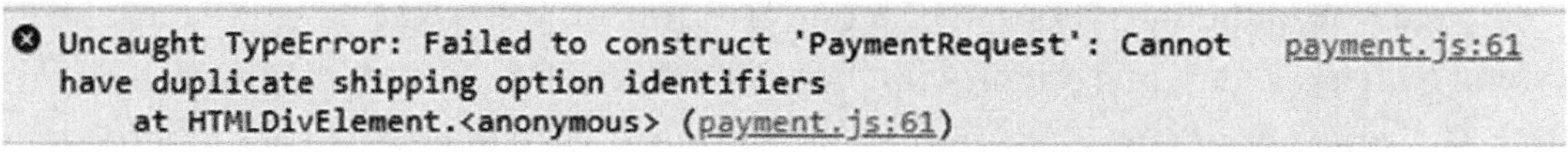

```
⊗ Uncaught TypeError: Failed to construct 'PaymentRequest': Cannot    payment.js:61
  have duplicate shipping option identifiers
      at HTMLDivElement.<anonymous> (payment.js:61)
```

Figure 4-14. *Duplicate IDs error*

Keep the terminal window open – we will make use of it throughout the rest of this exercise:

1. The next error we might see relates to a shipping object which is empty – for this, revert back to the payment.js file, and look for this line of code on or around line 65:

    ```
    }], shippingOptions: [{
    ```

2. This next change requires a little careful editing – remove the following code , as highlighted:

    ```
    }], shippingOptions: [{
      id: 'standard',
      label: 'FREE delivery (3-5 days)',
      amount: {currency: 'USD', value: '0.00'},
      selected: true,
    }, {
      id: 'express',
      label: 'Express delivery (next day)',
      amount: {currency: 'USD', value: '3.99'},
    },
      ],
    ```

3. Go ahead and preview the results as before, then add some products to the basket, and click Checkout securely.

What happens? We will find that the checkout form doesn't appear – instead, we will get the error shown in Figure 4-15 appear in the browser console:

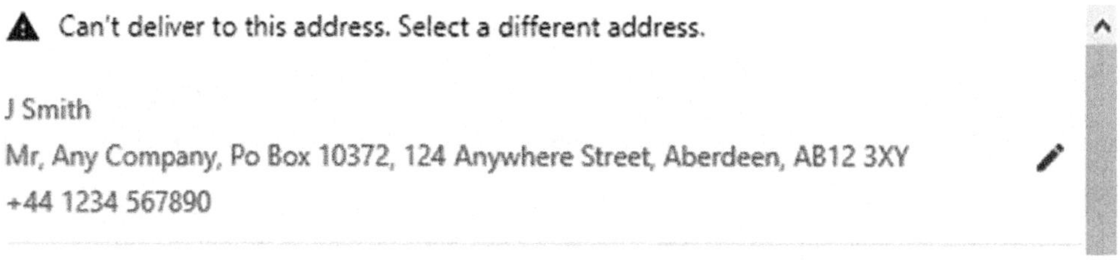

⚠ Can't deliver to this address. Select a different address.

J Smith

Mr, Any Company, Po Box 10372, 124 Anywhere Street, Aberdeen, AB12 3XY

+44 1234 567890

Figure 4-15. *Specifying an empty shippingOptions array*

1. The last error we're going to explore is what happens when you set an invalid shipping type. For this revert back to the `payment.js` file, then look for this line, on or around line 79:

    ```
    const paymentOptions = { requestPayerEmail: true, requestShipping:
    true };
    ```

2. At the moment, we're not specifying a value for `shippingType`, so let's say we wanted to use "collection". Go ahead and alter that line of code, as indicated:

    ```
    const paymentOptions = { requestPayerEmail: true, requestShipping:
    true, shippingType: "collection" };
    ```

3. Save the file then preview the results as before – it would be natural to assume that "collection" would be a good choice to display as part of the labels for delivery method and address, right?

Unfortunately, this is where the API would seem to disagree – instead of it displaying something like "Collection method", it throws an error similar to the one shown in Figure 4-16.

```
⊗ Uncaught TypeError: Failed to construct 'PaymentRequest': The        payment.js:80
  provided value 'collection' is not a valid enum value of type
  PaymentShippingType.
      at HTMLDivElement.<anonymous> (payment.js:80)
```

Figure 4-16. *The error we see when specifying an invalid shippingType value*

In this instance, the only values we can use are "delivery," "shipping," or "pickup" – this is clearly something we need to bear in mind when it comes to developing anything that uses the API!

All is not lost though – we can go some way to improving on at least one error that might be returned. If we wanted to, we can edit the last few lines of the `paymentDetails` constant to look like this:

```
    label: 'Sales Tax',
    amount: { currency: 'USD', value: tax.toFixed(2) }
  }],
  error: "Sorry - we can't deliver to that address.",
  shippingOptions: [],
};
```

We also need to remove the invalid shippingType entry – go ahead and delete the code highlighted here (from step 11 of the previous exercise):

```
const paymentOptions = { requestPayerEmail: true, requestShipping: true,
shippingType: "collection" };
```

If we were to save this and try to select an address, it will throw back the error shown in Figure 4-17 instead.

Figure 4-17. *Customizing at least one error message*

None of the errors we've covered are complicated – as long as we take care over how we plan the setup of the key parts such as the paymentDetails constant, then we should be able to steer clear of introducing them into our code. One in particular, the shipping type value, will affect how we set up our form; the others are just ones where we need to ensure that data being fed into the API has been sense-checked as part of the development process.

Summary

It goes without saying that shipping is equally key to the whole process as collecting payment; although we've only touched the surface of what might be possible in this regard, we've explored some useful tips to help get you started. Let's take a moment to review what we've learned in this chapter.

We kicked off by exploring how to choose the delivery address and set a default shipping option, before learning how to expand on these options so that we had something that more closely mirrored a real-world scenario.

We then moved onto examining how to react to changes made when selecting addresses or delivery methods, before understanding how to implement some basic restrictions on delivery, such as offering free postage for a restricted area. We then rounded out the chapter with a look at some of the typical errors we might see – we learned about how these may not all apply to shipping, but that some will – we then explored how to look out for some examples in a demo, and what we might expect to see if any do appear in our projects.

Our journey doesn't stop here though: we still have more to cover! Over the last few pages, we've covered a lot of detail about how to configure the form – it's time we took this up a notch and began to integrate a payment processor into the mix. There are dozens available, all offering different variations on the same theme; how we might choose one and integrate it will be the subject of the next chapter.

CHAPTER 5

Integrating with a Payment Handler

Anyone who knows me personally will know that I'm often in my local corner store – I've become something of a regular, having been visiting it regularly for over a decade. Over time, I've seen people walk up to the checkout, whip out their mobiles or even certain smart watches, and wave them past the credit card machine. Yep, the days of paying by card are numbered, or as some might say, fast becoming old-school!

But I digress – only partially though: the reason for talking about this is not only the use of near-field communications but also the use of services such as Google Pay, Apple Pay, and the like. I'll bet that unless you already happen to use one of these services to pay for goods at your nearest store, you'd be forgiven for thinking – "Google Pay"… "Android Pay"…"Microsoft Pay"…

What do they all offer? Do I use a merchant or payment provider? Who do I go with? Is one better than the other? All good questions – over the course of this chapter we'll explore all of these and more, so that you'll be able to make a more informed decision for your future projects. Let's make a start though, with a quick recap on some of the payment methods and concepts we need to be familiar with when using the API.

Exploring the Options

When working with the API, there are several key concepts we need to be aware of, which are:

- **Payment handlers** – behind each payment identifier is a payment handler – these are web-based or native payment applications that can be created by anyone who processes payments and which will store the customer's payment details and provide them to merchants at the point of authorization by the customer. Examples include Google Pay, Microsoft Pay, and Samsung Pay.

115

© Alex Libby 2019
A. Libby, *Checking Out with the Payment Request API*, https://doi.org/10.1007/978-1-4842-5184-3_5

We will explore how to create payment handlers in more detail as a project in Chapter 8, later in this book.

- **Payment instrument** – this is the generic name for each type of payment method, such as Google Pay, Microsoft Pay, or basic-card.

- **Basic-card** – this is a generic method of payment that is supported in the Payment Request API, accepts all credit or debit card types, and ideally should be set up as the default fallback option (if needed). It's designed for those who still want to use the API but are not yet ready to accept companies storing their details in a service such as Apple Pay.

- **Payment service provider (PSP)** – these are the companies who process payment requests and arrange transfer of funds from the customer to the merchant.

- **Payment identifiers** – these are strings such as basic-card or `https://google.com/pay`), which identify a payment method.

When we pay for goods online, we typically see a form asking for details as name, card number, and the like – this data is sent to a merchant on submission, who will process the payment on behalf of the customer.

In many cases, merchants will use the services of a payment service provider (PSP) to process that payment and make the money transfer. There are a host of different PSPs available; each work in their own way, but all of them can be integrated using one of the following three patterns:

API Type

The first of the three integration methods is the API type, where a merchant submits credit card information to their server through a form. This is sent onto the PSP using their API, for which the PSP will have a server-side SDK to help with implementing the service (Figure 5-1).

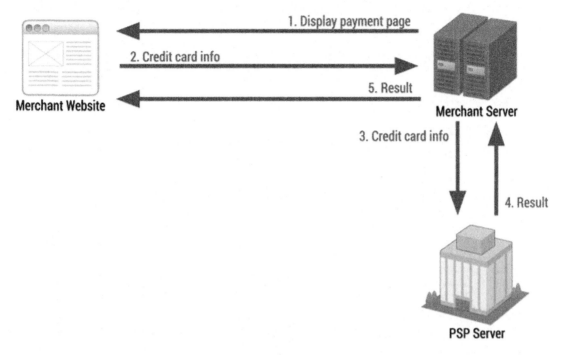

Figure 5-1. *API type method of integration*

This option is best suited for those developers who have a relatively strong technical skill set – this method is straightforward to implement but somewhat more complex than other integration methods such as Link type.

Link Type

In comparison, this next method, Link type, is the easiest to integrate – it's flexible design and less sophisticated user experience means that anyone can integrate a PSP into the Payment Request API using this method.

When a customer submits payment, the merchant forwards that customer to a PSP-hosted page with a form to accept credit card information. The details they then enter will be submitted directly to the PSP for processing – provided the payment is accepted, the customer will be brought back to the merchant web page to (hopefully) receive confirmation of a successful transaction, as shown in Figure 5-2.

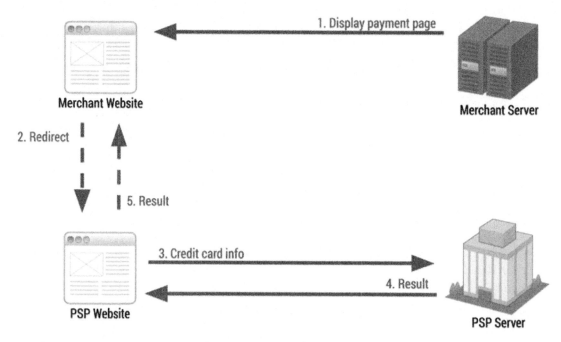

Figure 5-2. *The Link API method of integration*

Tokenization Type

The last method, Tokenization type, represents the most flexible and secure option – the payment form is shown in a page hosted on the merchant's site but served from a PSP's domain through an iframe (Figure 5-3).

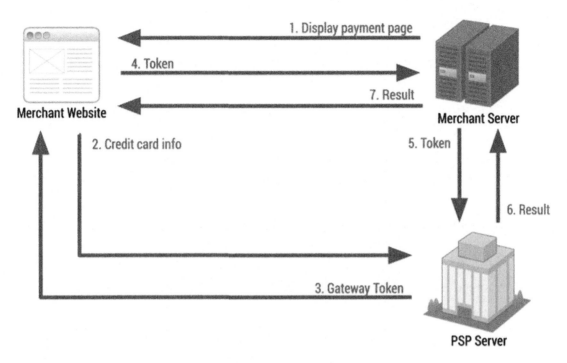

Figure 5-3. *The Tokenization type method of integration*

On submission, the customer's details are submitted directly to the PSP's server, and the merchant will receive a token as a result. The merchant can then verify it through their server and ask the PSP to process the payment.

This route offers the merchant a good mix of security, convenience, and design flexibility; most of the processes are handled by the PSP's client-side SDK. This allows the merchant to process payments without handling any of the client's credit or debit card details during the process.

Integrating with the Payment Request API

Although we've covered three different types of integration, in reality we may only be able to use two of them. The two we can choose from are the API and Tokenization methods; the decoupled design of Link type is such that it precludes the use of the Payment Request API, as API calls must be deferred to the PSP to process.

- **API type** – although this is the easiest method to use (where we receive the information, parse it and forward it to the PSP), it requires PCI compliance, at SAQ A-EP or DSS level, as you are handling raw credit card information. This may preclude all except those who are sufficiently large, can afford to, and make a concerted effort to achieve PCI compliance.

- **Tokenization type** – this method relies on sending payment details to the PSP server and receiving a token in return. Although it removes some of the need to handle credit card information, it still requires PCI compliance. It's a combination of needing to satisfy the minimum level of PCI compliance needed (PCI SAQ-A) yet remove the need for merchants to touch sensitive information and still integrate it into their system, which makes this method complex and harder to implement.

You can learn more about PCI compliance at `https://www.pcicompliance guide.org`.

Although we've covered the three different types of integration and seen how using the Payment Request API may affect our choices, many payment processors provide options which abstract away much of the technical considerations. This therefore makes it easier to implement a solution using the Payment Request API; we still have to be mindful of concerns such as PCI compliance, but the work required may not be so onerous, depending on which solution we decide to implement in our projects.

Choosing between a PSP or Traditional Provider

Once we've decided on our preferred integration route, the next decision to make is whether to use a traditional merchant or payment service provider (PSP). Integrating a provider into the Payment Request API requires a whole series of decisions to be made – the outcome of which will affect how successful your site is with customers. Both process payments, so what is the difference, and why would we choose one over the other? At a basic level, both process payments, but there are some key differences which are highlighted in Table 5-1.

Table 5-1. *Differences between merchant and PSP accounts*

Merchant account	Account with PSP
Account is held directly with the service provider, which can typically be a bank or financial institution.	Account held with PSP, who acts on behalf of multiple providers – this makes it more flexible and can help reduce the amount of work required to implement a solution.
Fees are more expensive.	Fees generally lower – most do not charge monthly recurring subscriptions.
Accounts will be more robust and likely require more work to integrate into an existing site.	Accounts can be less robust than traditional merchants; integration is easier to manage.
Better suited for those who will make substantial revenue – this would likely be above £5,000 per annum.	Suited more for retailers who don't make substantial revenue.

So how do we decide between either type? Much of this will depend on the nature of your projects – both types will be subject to some form of regulation by the relevant financial authority for your country and will offer a number of common features such as card security, acceptance of different card types, reporting, and technical support.

To help narrow down the choices though, there are some key questions we should ask ourselves:

- Payments made by PSPs are instantaneous, whereas income from sales made through standard merchants can typically take a few days; is the size of your business such that this delay (and associated risk of non-payment) might affect your survival?

- If the size of your business is such that you do not have the staff available to manually deal with accounting/banking, then the instantaneous payments offered by PSPs could be a real benefit.

- Although it is straightforward to set up a suitable account for credit and debit card payments, it can take some time to get approval – any delay in receiving income can have a detrimental effect on the bottom line.

- PSPs offer the ability for merchants to accept multiple payment methods, whereas traditional providers may offer a more limited choice; research has shown that customers prefer having choice and that a lack of choice may put customers off from buying products from your company.

- PSPs offer the ability to make payments from any location, irrespective of borders – this includes those customers who don't have a bank account.

- PSPs offer the ability to accept payments in local currencies – when working with a traditional provider, accounts have to be set up for each currency, which can become costly to manage. PSPs have connections with local acquiring banks for your country and so can offer this facility more easily than through traditional means. What's more, offering support for local currencies can save the retailer from paying conversion fees, costs which otherwise would have to be recouped from customers!

Judging by some of these questions, it would seem that going with a PSP could be very beneficial and that one might ask what the future holds for more traditional providers!

The API is still very young though, and that for legal or financial reasons, using the Payment Request API may not suit companies who work in a B2B environment if they have to collect extra details – for example, Italian companies have to collect IVA details (VAT tax number for Italy). It is possible though that once the API has become more mainstream, some of the older providers are forced to refocus what they offer, so it works through the API, and not just as a standalone offer.

Okay, so I digress – time to bring things back to the present, methinks! Let us for the purposes of this book assume that we've decided to go with a PSP. Question is – who? Well, there are plenty of providers available worldwide; this is where names such as Apple Pay, Microsoft Pay, Google Pay, or even Amazon Pay come into their own. Some of the more traditional providers such as WorldPay do offer services that include the likes of Apple Pay, but this tends to be limited, and that they focus more on their own offerings instead.

A more effective solution would be to go with a PSP that can offer services that are compatible with multiple partners; this will save both development time and resource, as a single integration will automatically handle payment for the selected payment method, without the need to set up a separate facility. A good example of this is Stripe, who have multiple offices throughout Europe, Asia, and the United States – they offer a service called Stripe Elements, which is perfect for working with the Request API. In fact, if you look closely at their code (which we'll cover in the next but one exercise), you can begin to see some terms which should begin to look very familiar...

Implementing a Provider

We've talked briefly about how using the services of a PSP such as Stripe will help simplify matters (as well as time and cost), but before we dive into their code, I have a small confession to make: we won't be able to create a *fully working* version of their code in this book.

Now – before you all jump up and try to throttle me, there is good reason for this: Stripe uses an API key which has to be inserted into the code for it to work properly. For reasons of security, I'm not going to be able to include one in our next demo, but we can at least do the next best thing: we'll work through a live example on Stripe's web site, explore how we would set up Stripe for our own projects, and use an alternative payment app so you can get a feel for how things will operate.

To make a start, we'll first set up a test payment app called BobPay – this has been designed for use with systems such as the Payment Request API, so you'll get a feel for how things should work when using a payment app with the standard basic-card option in a checkout form. Let's take a look at this in more detail:

ADDING IN BOBPAY

For this demo, we'll be using a copy of the bobpay folder from the code download that accompanies this book – make sure you save a copy to our project area, before continuing with these steps:

1. We'll start by first visiting the BobPay web site at `https://bobpay.xyz` – go ahead and click the link marked "Install BobPay Web Payment App" toward the bottom of the page.

2. Next, open a copy of payment.js in your usual text editor – the first few lines contain the `paymentMethods` constant.

3. Go ahead and add in the code highlighted below, then save the file.

```
window.onload = function(e) {
  const paymentMethods = [{
    supportedMethods: 'basic-card',
    data: {
      supportedNetworks: ['visa', 'mastercard', 'amex']
    }
  }, {
    supportedMethods: 'https://bobpay.xyz/pay'
  }, {
    supportedMethods: 'interledger'
  }];
```

4. We can now preview the results of our work, so in order to do this, fire up a
    Node.js terminal session and change the working directory to the bobpay
    folder within our project area.

5. At the prompt, go ahead and enter this command:

```
ws -hostname localhost --https
```

6. If we browse to https://localhost:8000/index.html to preview the
    results, then add in some products to our basket, and hit Checkout securely, we
    will see our updated default shipping option (Figure 5-4).

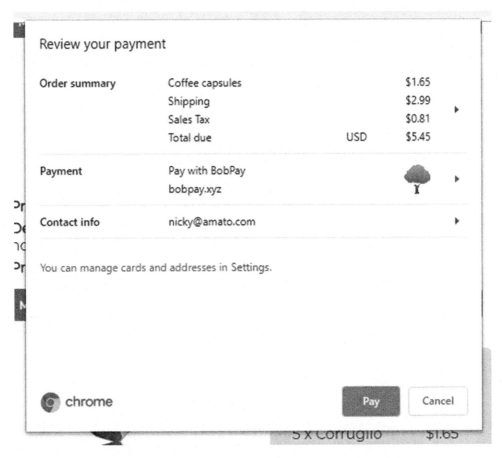

Figure 5-4. *BobPay implemented using the API*

7. Hit Pay – on the next screen, you will see this:

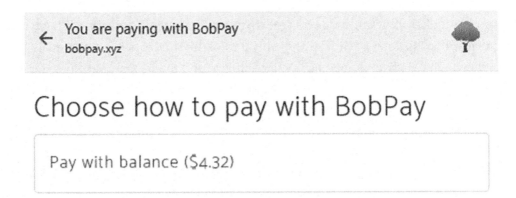

Figure 5-5. *Paying with BobPay...*

8. BobPay will show a fake balance amount – if you click Details at the bottom of the screen, you will see a JSON object with details of the purchase, including total cost.

9. Hit the Pay with balance ($4.32) button – the form will disappear, and the API will show that payment has been received after a few seconds (this will take longer to complete, when running in a production environment.)

10. At this point, fire up your browser's DOM inspector – if all is well, you will see a response, akin to the details shown in Figure 5-6.

```
{"requestId":"3fa60aab-569c-4ed7-867e-d38c9bb5cf72","methodName":"https://bob payment.js:61
pay.xyz/pay","details":{"token_id":"ABCDEADBEEF","message":"Amount deducted from
balance"},"shippingAddress":null,"shippingOption":null,"payerName":null,"payerEmail":"y@t","
payerPhone":null}
>
```

Figure 5-6. *The results of the BobPay request*

This was an easy change to make, but nevertheless an important one – it shows how in reality, we might have several methods available to us, when it comes to selecting how we pay for products. It's important to note that BobPay is purely a representation of how things will look when developing the production version of our site; there are a few important concepts we should explore, so let's take a moment to dive into our code in more detail, and what this means for us.

Dissecting the Code

Take another look back at the code changes we made in payment.js – although we only added in less than six lines of code, this is only part of the story. Let me explain:

Payment apps, such as Google Pay, Microsoft Pay, and the like, are supported in the Payment Request API but are not enabled by default. Adding in the six lines of code at the start of payment.js was only the beginning; when we visited the BobPay web site and clicked "Install BobPay Web Payment App," this installed something called a payment handler.

In short, these store the credit or debit card details for a customer and are sent to the processor for payment, once authorization has been given by the customer. In our example, we've provided details for both basic-card, BobPay, and interledger (the latter is just another payment app that can be used through the API). This is done using the `supportedMethods` parameter in each instance; we also provide some additional details such as supported cards using the `supportedNetworks` attribute.

Creating such a handler is a little complicated – suffice to say that these each represent a payment method (such as Google Pay), although a handler can be shared between multiple apps. To make things easier, we'll keep to a one-to-one relationship; the former is something to bear once you are more accustomed to using payment handlers.

Understanding the Types of Payment Identifiers

Now that we've begun to talk about using payment handlers, it's time we explored what these are – they come in two different guises: standardized and URL-based.

You will already be familiar with the first type, although perhaps not realize it – the basic-card method we've used is supported in all browsers that implement the Payment Request API.

It's fine for testing, but as it contains raw credit card data, this is a high security risk which means it is not something we will continue to use forever! Suffice to say that if you needed to use this format, you will definitely have to invest in PCI DSS compliance, which can be costly and may not be worth the resource and time required for your organization.

There are other standardized candidates that are or have been under discussion, such as basic credit transfer (to transfer between bank accounts – see `https://w3c.github.io/payment-method-credit-transfer/`) or Interledger payment method, using the Interledger protocol (`https://interledger.org/`).

The second type, URL-based payments, can be defined independently and do not fall under the auspices of the W3C; these contain a specific URL identifier, such as Google Pay (`https://google.com/pay`). These methods can be shared across multiple payment apps and can be created by anyone with an interest in handling payments – the latter makes it easy to scale up services offered to retailers very easily.

At this point, I'm going to flip things on their head – we can always decide to go with a specific payment method directly, such as Google Pay; nothing wrong with this approach, right?

Well, yes – and no. Yes, there is nothing wrong *technically*, but it's not the best route from a practical perspective. Why? Simple – what about those people who don't use your chosen method? You will have to incorporate multiple payment methods, which brings an overhead in time and resources to manage.

The more effective method is to use a PSP, as we talked about earlier – this allows us to combine several payment methods such as Google Pay or Apple Pay into one unified interface. A great example of this is Stripe, who have offices in multiple locations worldwide and so can help support payments in multiple currencies, local language support, and so on – this will be a real boon. Over the course of the next few pages, we're going to take a look at how we might implement Stripe and see that it works in a similar way to the standard Payment Request API.

Implementing Stripe

At this point, I have a small confession to make – for reasons of security and logistics, we're not going to be able to create a fully working demo.

To get around this, we will work through the current steps that are required to set up Stripe to use the Payment Request API and explore how it works in action through one of their demos. Hopefully by the end of this demo, it will give you a flavor of how we might implement the API using a PSP, and that with care, it should not be difficult to implement a basic system to get you started in your site.

Note   If you want to use Stripe in your projects, it's worth noting that new forthcoming regulations (the Strong Customer Authentication, or SCA) will require additional changes for European businesses. To reflect this, we will use the Payment Intents API system offered by Stripe, which is compatible with the SCA.

As an aside – you may also find CodePen demos online too, which show you the basics of using Stripe; in the interests of fair play, I won't list any here, but if you search for "codepen stripe.js demos" using Google, you should find a good few examples to have a look at during development.

For this next exercise, we're going to do something a little different – this time around, we'll walk through using Stripe's Payment Request API demo, so we can see how it works in practice, and that the code used follows the same principle themes as our code.

Note   For those interested in exploring more at the end of this walk-through, the source code is available on Stripe's GitHub site for this demo, which is at `https://github.com/stripe/stripe-payments-demo`.

WALK-THROUGH: ADDING IN STRIPE

The demo in question is available at `https://stripe-payments-demo.appspot.com/` – browse to this first, before you follow through with these steps:

1. We're only interested in the purple button at the top (marked Pay Now), so go ahead and click on it – you will see the by now familiar Payment Request API window appear; it will likely have a few defaults already set, depending on what you have set in your browser. It will look similar to the screenshot shown in Figure 5-7.

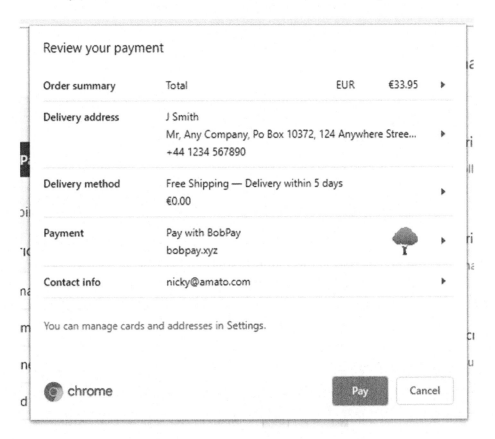

Figure 5-7. *Stripe's Payment Request API example*

If you don't see the window show, make sure you have some dummy credit card/
debit card details and addresses set in your browser; there are plenty of sites
online that can help generate these details if you're stuck for inspiration!

2. Try changing the selected card, by clicking the right arrow by Payment, then
    selecting Add Card – it gives an example card at the bottom of the main page.

3. Click back to the main screen, then click Pay and add in the CVC number (any
    will do) – stripe will pause for a moment to simulate processing, then display a
    "Thanks for your order!" message to confirm a successful transaction.

The demo by Stripe shows off perfectly how we can use the Payment Request API,
and that we can create a consistent checkout process with the minimum of code, instead
of creating a monolithic cart that takes resource time and effort to manage.

This allows us to focus more on the various payment methods we want to support
in our site, and how we manage these through our cart, as well as providing the relevant
details. With this in mind, let's take a quick look at the code Stripe have used for the
demo; you should start to see similarities with code we've created in earlier demos!

Breaking Apart the Code

At this point I know what you might well want to ask – what was the point of that
exercise? It's a fair question: we didn't do a great deal and certainly nothing different to
what we've done in our own demos from earlier in the book.

That, my friends, was the point of the demo: using a PSP may require writing
different code, but this should be for handling changes and exceptions, not for the
basic checkout. The instance of the Payment Request API that Stripe has set up looks
no different – granted it uses different card details, but the look and feel of the cart itself
should be consistent, no matter how you integrate it into your site.

The real area of interest though is the `payments.js` file they've created (yes, it is
just coincidental that it's the same name as the ones we've created!). I would strongly
recommend saving a copy from `https://stripe-payments-demo.appspot.com/`
`javascripts/payments.js` and opening this in a decent text editor; it will make life
easier when we look at the code.

Much of this code is for the Stripe Elements form that you saw during the walk-through – the code of interest to us starts on or around line 128, with this comment: Implement a Stripe Payment Request Button Element.

The first block at line 139 initiates an instance of the Payment Request API – into this we provide the `country`, `currency` to use, `total` (`amount` and `label`), as well as `request` `shipping` and `email` details.

The next block (from line 152 onward), takes care of instances where payment methods are added such as new credit cards; this request then updates the `PaymentIntent` request which Stripe uses (we touched on this updated version earlier). We then perform a similar update if the shipping address is changed; this just acknowledges the change.

The next block from line 193 looks after any changes made to shipping options – we use `event.updateWith()` (which we've touched on before), to reflect changes back to the totals displayed in our checkout. The last two blocks then display the Payment Request API button, based on whether the browser supports it and that there is at least one payment method available for us to use.

Note   If you are interested in learning more about how Stripe works with the Payment Request API, please refer to their documentation at `https://stripe.com/docs/payment-request-api`.

This got me thinking – if we applied Stripe to one of our earlier demos, say the chillis one from Chapter 2, how would it look? This is a good question – fortunately it's easy enough to mock up something that answers this question; it's not perfect, but it will give you a flavor of what to expect if you decide to use a PSP such as Stripe.

Making it More Local

You must forgive the somewhat odd title to this next section – it is a little contrived, but the "local" is a reference to creating something that can run locally rather than remotely!

While researching for this book, I spent some time mocking up changes to the original chilli demo we created back in Chapter 2 – I wanted to keep things simple, so that you can see how easy it is to integrate a system from a PSP such as Stripe into an existing site. A couple of hours work, and a few coffees later, an updated version was born: the results are shown in Figure 5-8.

Cart

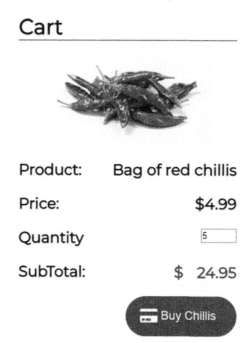

Product: Bag of red chillis

Price: $4.99

Quantity   5

SubTotal: $ 24.95

Buy Chillis

Figure 5-8. *A mock up using Stripe.js*

As you can see from the screenshot, it doesn't look that different! This is deliberate – had we had to make wholesale changes to the overall design, then this is a good indication that it's not fit for purpose, and changing it will likely have a negative impact on the experience for customers. Indeed, the only noticeable change is the credit card symbol appearing in the button (and possibly that the text size is a little smaller there too); the overall experience will remain the same.

To achieve this, I made some changes to the HTML markup – primarily to introduce that credit card symbol but also to add a slot to display the token response we get back from Stripe.

The real changes though come in the scripts.js file; the code is completely rewritten from ground up. Let's take a look at the updated version block by block, starting with declaring some variables:

```
(function () {
  // Switch out the test key here with your own
  let stripe = Stripe('<ENTER API KEY HERE>');
  let paymentRequest = stripe.paymentRequest({
      country: 'US',
```

```
    currency: 'usd',
    total: {
      label: 'Total to pay',
      amount: 2495,
    },
    requestPayerName: true,
    requestPayerEmail: true,
    requestShipping: true,
    shippingOptions: [
    {
      id: 'free-shipping',
      label: 'Free shipping',
      detail: 'Arrives in 5 to 7 days',
      amount: 0,
    },
  ],
});
```

In this block, we're declaring our initial PaymentRequest object; we provide basic details such as total cost, label, and requests for the payer's name, email, and shipping details. Although the format looks different, the same terminology has been used here as we've already used before; this will help with the integration.

```
// Check the availability of the Payment Request API first.
paymentRequest.canMakePayment().then(function(result) {
  let button = document.getElementById('payment-request-button');
  if (result) {
    button.style.display = 'inline-block';
    button.addEventListener('click', paymentRequest.show);
  } else {
    button.style.display = 'none';
  }
});
```

This next block controls whether we display the pay button – again, this will be very similar to what we've created before. In particular, note the use of `Promise()` terminology such as `.then()` – this is identical to what we've already created.

```
  paymentRequest.on('token', function(ev) {
    document.getElementById('payment-token').innerText = ev.token.id;
    document.getElementById('payment-token-message').style.display =
    'block';

    ev.complete('success');
  });
})();
```

In the final block, we display a token that is returned from Stripe, to confirm success; the token can then be used by us for further processing. At this stage, we would render a suitable message on screen to confirm the outcome of the purchase; we must though mark the Payment Request API part of the process as complete before completing our part of the overall transaction.

In comparison, have a look at some example Payment Request API code, written for incorporating Google Pay directly into a site:

```
const googlePayPaymentMethod = {
  supportedMethods: 'https://google.com/pay',
  data: {
    'environment': 'TEST',
    'apiVersion': 1,
    'allowedPaymentMethods': ['CARD', 'TOKENIZED_CARD'],
    'paymentMethodTokenizationParameters': {
      'tokenizationType': 'PAYMENT_GATEWAY',
      'parameters': {}
    },
    'cardRequirements': {
      'allowedCardNetworks': ['AMEX', 'DISCOVER', 'MASTERCARD', 'VISA'],
      'billingAddressRequired': true,
      'billingAddressFormat': 'MIN'
    },
    'phoneNumberRequired': true,
    'emailRequired': true,
    'shippingAddressRequired': true
  },
};
```

Source: Google

While there is technically nothing wrong with this approach, if this is the only payment method that is plumbed into the API, we would miss out on those customers who prefer using the likes of other clients such as Apple Pay or even Microsoft Pay! This is one good reason why using a PSP is frequently more beneficial than plumbing in payment handlers directly into our code.

Dealing with Extra Charges

Throughout the course of this book, we've explored some useful features that we can add to our checkout form, to help fine-tune the journey for our customers. Some were small, such as updating the button text, to much larger ones such as implementing discounts – nevertheless all are just as important.

However, this next change may bring us back to reality with something of a bump – implementing extra charges. No one likes them, but retailers will say they have to cover costs; trouble is, some are likely to try to justify higher charges that don't necessarily reflect the real cost of the service! The typical one is credit cards; for this, we might expect to pay a percentage increase on top of the total amount, to reflect the processing costs involved (and some might also argue, reflect the risk).

No matter what the reason for the charge is, implementing it is very easy and requires us to modify the payment details object we set up for the API. The W3C's specification looks like this:

```
dictionary PaymentDetailsModifier {
    required DOMString supportedMethods;
    PaymentItem total;
    sequence<PaymentItem> additionalDisplayItems;
    object data;
};
```

At first glance, this looks a little complicated but in reality, it's easier than it looks – take a look at this example:

```
modifiers: [{
    supportedMethods: 'https://bobpay.xyz/pay',
    additionalDisplayItems: [{
```

```
          label: 'Processing fee',
          amount: { currency: 'USD', value: '3.00' }
        }],
      total: {
        label: 'Total to pay by card',
        amount: {currency: 'USD', value: Number(total + 3).toFixed(2)}}
      }],
```

If we break it apart, it resembles something of a mix between the paymentMethods and paymentDetails objects we've created for previous demos. The first section simply states the final amount to be charged, but the section in bold is key: we have to specify which payment methods are affected, as well as what the extra charge or discount is (additionalDisplayItems[]), and how this affects the overall total to be charged to our customer.

The best way to understand what this means is to see it in action – without further ado, let's implement an example in our next demo, where we apply a small processing charge for those customers who prefer to use credit cards. Beware though – there is something of a sting in this proverbial tale; I will reveal all after this next exercise.

CREDIT CARD CHARGES

For this demo, we'll use a copy of the bobpay folder we updated earlier in this chapter – save this as charges, at the root of our project folder. Make sure also that you've still got the payment handler for BobPay installed; have a quick check to see what it says at the bottom of the BobPay web site, if you are unsure.

Assuming both are in place, let's make a start with the demo:

1. We'll begin by opening a copy of payment.js from within the charges folder – look for label: 'Sales Tax', which will be on or around line 48.

2. Go ahead and add in the following (highlighted) code as indicated below:

```
     label: 'Sales Tax',
     amount: { currency: 'USD', value: tax.toFixed(2) }
   }],
   modifiers: [{
     supportedMethods: 'https://bobpay.xyz/pay',
```

```
        additionalDisplayItems: [{
        label: 'Processing fee',
        amount: { currency: 'USD', value: '3.00' }
    }],
    total: {
        label: 'Total to pay by card',
        amount: {currency: 'USD', value: Number(total + 3).toFixed(2)}}
    }],
};
```

3. Go ahead and save the file – we can now preview the results of our work, so in order to do this, fire up a Node.js terminal session and change the working directory to the bobpay folder within our project area.

4. At the prompt, go ahead and enter this command:

```
ws -hostname localhost --https
```

5. If we browse to `https://localhost:8000/index.html` to preview the results, then add in some products to our basket and hit Checkout securely, we will see our checkout cart, with BobPay highlighted as the chosen payment method (Figure 5-9):

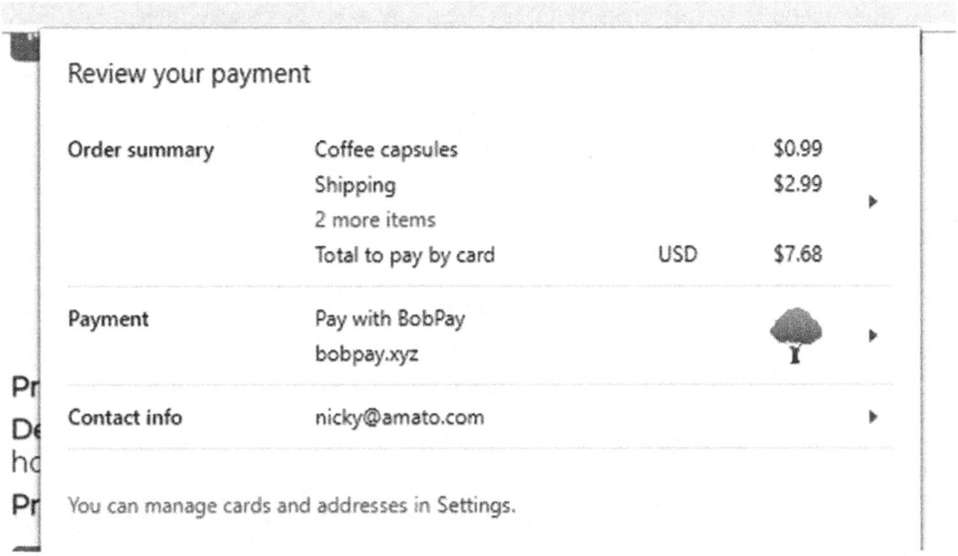

Review your payment

Order summary	Coffee capsules		$0.99
	Shipping		$2.99
	2 more items		
	Total to pay by card	USD	$7.68
Payment	Pay with BobPay		
	bobpay.xyz		
Contact info	nicky@amato.com		

You can manage cards and addresses in Settings.

Figure 5-9. *Our checkout form, with extra items present...*

6. A quick click on the arrow to the right of the order summary should reveal that we do indeed have an extra processing fee being applied (Figure 5-10).

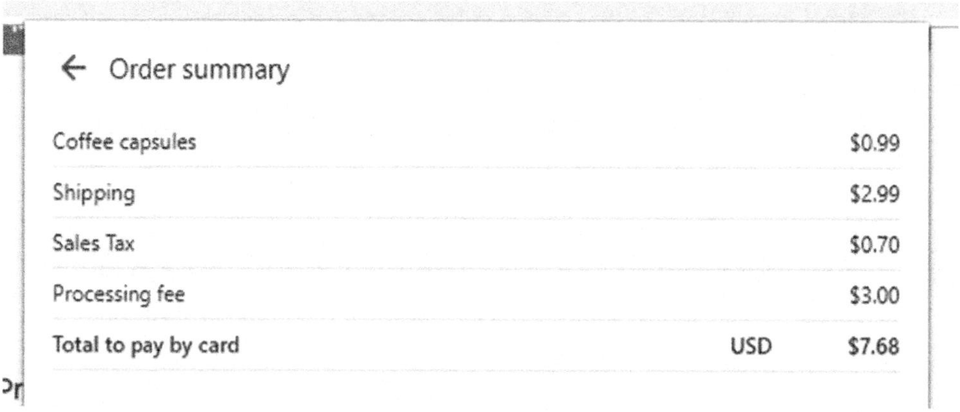

← Order summary		
Coffee capsules		$0.99
Shipping		$2.99
Sales Tax		$0.70
Processing fee		$3.00
Total to pay by card	USD	$7.68

Figure 5-10. *A processing fee applied when using BobPay*

7. Try choosing another payment method – hopefully by now you will at least have a basic-card method available; if not, click Payment (from the previous screen), then Add Card to add in suitable details.

8. Assuming we've selected a different method, we should see less items appear in the summary; a click on the next screen will also confirm that when using basic-card, we're not applying any extra processing fees (Figure 5-11).

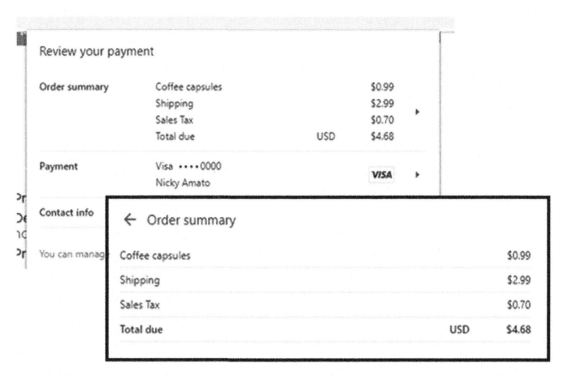

Figure 5-11. *No processing fees applied when using basic-card*

As this demo shows, it is very easy to apply additional charges when using a particular method of payment. However, while it may technically easy to do this, there are at least two critical points which we should be aware of, if we decide to add charges; let's take a look at both these and our code in more detail, to understand why things may not be as straightforward as they may first appear!

Breaking Apart the Code in Detail

At the start of this exercise, I did warn of a sting in this tale – and with good reason: there are two good reasons for not applying charges, unless you absolutely have to! Let me explain what I mean:

The first one is that although the `PaymentDetailsModifier` feature has been in browsers for a while (e.g., it came in Chrome 62), it has nevertheless had something of a checkered history. Tests and comments made on the W3C GitHub site for Payment Request API indicate that performance is inconsistent; indications are that support for it will likely be altered to only work with external networks. It's for this reason that our demo is only set to apply the extra three-dollar charge when using BobPay; this is not applied when using basic-card.

There is a wider concern though – depending on where you live, you may find that it will (if not already has) become illegal to apply extra charges in your country. A good example of this is applying extra charges when certain types of cards are used for payment online, such as credit cards (whereas debit cards do not incur this charge). There are two reasons for this: a lack of transparency will put customers off, and that some retailers add charges that don't reflect the true cost of using that service to them. In some senses, it's better to just steer clear of applying charges unless you absolutely have to; it is much safer to incorporate the charges into other items so their cost is covered!

That aside, setting up the charge feature is very straightforward – we include all of the details within a modifiers section at the end of the `paymentDetails` constant. We first specify which `supportedMethods` should be included; in this case it is just BobPay. We then add in an `additionalDisplayItems` property, which states what is being added and how much it is. This is then finished with the `total` property that states the `label` to use and what the final `amount` to the customer will be. As in previous exercises, we can add up values from elsewhere in the cart to arrive at the total figure.

Okay – let's move on: there's one more feature we should cover, when dealing with payment exceptions; what happens if our customer doesn't have a payment app installed? Without one they clearly can't take advantage of the quick checkout process; we should make sure they can easily add something in! Let's take a look at how we might achieve this, and what it means for the customer, in more detail.

Dealing with No Payment Apps

The days of using a traditional credit card are fast disappearing – systems such as Apple Pay and Google Pay make it a real snap to effect payment for those retailers who support it via their web site.

However, I know there will be moments when we don't have a particular payment app installed, such as Apple Pay – instead of simply dropping customers out (and incurring a few choice words in the process!), we can affect a very simple change that will encourage them to go and install that payment app.

Granted, customers may still choose to go elsewhere, but at least we give them the opportunity to carry on, and not simply drop them at the first point of failure. That aside, let's take a look at the steps involved to effect this change:

NO PAYMENT APPS PRESENT

For this demo, we'll need a copy of the nobob folder – go ahead and save a copy of this as nobob in our project area, before you continue with these steps:

1. First, go ahead and open `index.html` in your text editor – look for the closing `</div>` on line 61, and add or edit the following as indicated:

   `<div class="paylabel">Checkout securely with:</div>`
   `<div class="pay-button">`**`Credit Card`**`</div>`
   `<div class="pay-bob"><span class="img"></span>BobPay</div>`

2. Next, go ahead and grab a copy of the bobpay.png image from the images folder within the nobob folder in the accompanying download – drop this into the images folder within the nobob folder at the root of our project area.

3. We now need to add in some styles to adjust how the buttons and label look in the HTML markup. For this, go ahead and open `styles.css` in the nobob folder within the project area, then edit the `.pay-button` style rules as indicated:

   ```
   .pay-button, .pay-bob {
     width: 210px;
   ....
   }

   .pay-button:hover, .pay-bob:hover {
     cursor: pointer;
   }
   ```

4. Leave a line, then add in these three rules below:

   ```
   .pay-bob > .img { background: url(../images/bobpay.png) no-repeat;
   height: 30px; width: 40px; display: inline-block;  margin-top: 1px;
   vertical-align: bottom; }

   .paylabel { padding: 15px 0 0 0; }
   ```

5. We can close this file – next, open `scripts.js`, and add the following in at line 11:

```
paybobEl = document.querySelector(".pay-bob"),
paylabelEl = document.querySelector(".paylabel");
```

6. Next, add in the highlighted lines on or around line 90:

```
    paymentEl.style.display = "block";
    paybobEl.style.display = "block";
    paylabelEl.style.display = "block";
    totalPriceEl.innerHTML = calculateTotalPrice();
  } else {
    emptyCartEl.style.display = "none";
    cartCheckoutEl.style.display = "none";
    paymentEl.style.display = "none";
    paybobEl.style.display = "none";
    paylabelEl.style.display = "none";
  }
}
```

7. We're almost done with the editing – we need to modify the contents of `payment.js`, so go ahead and open this file in your text editor.

8. The first change we make here will be to delete lines 2 to 11, and replace with this block of code:

```
const payCardMethods = [{
    supportedMethods: 'basic-card',
    data: {
      supportedNetworks: ['visa', 'mastercard', 'amex']
    }
  }];

  const payBobMethods = [{
    supportedMethods: 'https://localhost:8000/pay'
  }];
```

9. Next, in line 36 change the word `paymentDetails` to `payCardDetails`.

10. Now go ahead and change `paymentOptions` in line 53 to `payCardOptions`.

11. In line 54, alter the properties passed into the Payment Request call, to reflect the changes made earlier in the file – this line should now read thus:

```
let request = new PaymentRequest(payCardMethods, payCardDetails,
payCardOptions);
```

12. Look for the `err.message` code in line 64, and change as highlighted:

```
}).catch(function(err) {
  if (err.code == DOMException.ABORT_ERR) {
```

13. The last big change is to add in a new event handler for the button we created earlier in the exercise – this will call a separate instance of Payment Request API, which is linked solely to the BobPay payment method. From line 83 onwards, add in the following code – we'll do this block by block, as there is a fair chunk to work through, starting with the opening declarations:

```
document.querySelector(".pay-bob").addEventListener("click",
function(e) {
    document.getElementById("message").className = ";

    if (window.PaymentRequest) {
      let subtotal = Number(document.querySelector(".total-price").
      innerText);
      let shipping = 2.99;
      let tax = (subtotal + shipping) * 0.175;
      let total = Number(subtotal) + Number(tax) + Number(shipping);

      const payBobDetails = {
        total: {
          label: 'Total due',
          amount: { currency: 'USD', value:  total.toFixed(2) }
        },
        displayItems: [{
          label: 'Coffee capsules',
          amount: { currency: 'USD', value: subtotal.toFixed(2) }
        },{
          label: 'Shipping',
          amount: { currency: 'USD', value: 2.99 }
        }, {
```

```
      label: 'Sales Tax',
      amount: { currency: 'USD', value: tax.toFixed(2) }
   }],
};

const payBobOptions = { requestPayerEmail: true };
let request = new PaymentRequest(payBobMethods, payBobDetails,
payBobOptions);
```

14. Next, immediately add in the core function that initiates the Payment Request API, provided the browser supports it:

```
if (request.canMakePayment) {
  request.canMakePayment().then(function(result) {
    request.show().then(function(result) {
      result.complete('success').then(function() {
        console.log(JSON.stringify(result));
        displaySuccess();
      });
    }).catch(function(err) {
      if (err.code == DOMException.ABORT_ERR) {
        displayMessage("Request has been cancelled");
      } else {
        displayError();
        console.log('Cannot make payment');
      }

      if (err.code == DOMException.NOT_SUPPORTED_ERR) {
        displayMessage("Sorry - BobPay isn't installed:
        redirecting...");
        setTimeout(function() {
          window.location.href = 'https://bobpay.xyz/#download';
        }, 5000)
      }
    });
  });
}
});
```

15. Go ahead and save all of your files then close them – we can now preview the results of our work. In order to do this, fire up a Node.js terminal session and change the working directory to the nobob folder within our project area.

16. At the prompt, go ahead and enter this command:

    ```
    ws -hostname localhost --https
    ```

17. If we browse to `https://localhost:8000/index.html` to preview the results, then add in some products to our basket, and hit Checkout securely, we will see the error message shown in Figure 5-12, before it redirects to the BobPay web site.

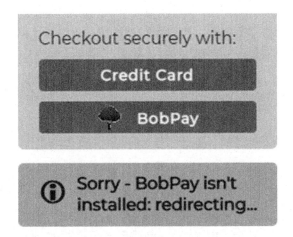

Figure 5-12. *An indication that BobPay is not installed…*

Although this seemed like a lot of steps to work through, the reality is that the change itself is minimal; it goes to show that we can definitely do more than simply drop customers out of the payment process at the first hurdle! The extra steps we covered afforded us an opportunity to tidy up the code and include some cleaner error handling – let's take a moment to review what we've created in more detail.

Understanding What Happened

Our somewhat lengthy demo didn't go into detail as to what happened in each step – exploring each part in turn wouldn't make sense until everything was put together as the final article. We've made a fair few changes, so let's explore these in turn:

The first change we made concerned our markup – we needed to create a separate instance of the Payment Request API, so you could see more clearly what happens. For this, we needed a new button using standard markup; it made better sense to also include a new label so that we could keep the important button text short.

The next changes came in the `script.js` file – for this, we had to hide the new button and label initially (done via CSS); these were then revealed as soon as items were added to our basket. The last set of changes concerned the payment.js file, where we duplicated the original instance of the Payment Request API and tied this to the new button created in our initial markup. In the main, this is largely identical to the existing instance; nevertheless, we had to alter the names so that each instance called the correct properties such as `paymentMethods`, `paymentDetails` and `paymentOptions`.

The real crux of the code changes though, centers around this extract:

```
if (err.code == DOMException.NOT_SUPPORTED_ERR) {
  displayMessage("Sorry - BobPay isn't installed: redirecting...");
  setTimeout(function() {
    window.location.href = 'https://bobpay.xyz/#download';
  }, 5000)
}
```

This is what makes the whole demo work – we're using the `DOMException` object to trap for errors and redirect if it detects that the payment app is not supported (i.e. not installed). As this is a better way to trap than simply capturing the text of the error (which we did in the original BobPay demo), we also took the opportunity to clean up some of the error handling to make for a cleaner, more accurate experience for our customers.

Checking for No Apps: An Epilogue

At first glance, you may not have noticed a small but critical change in our `payment.js` file, when compared to the original version used in the BobPay demo.

We've not included some lines of code in the nobob version in the text, but if you take a look at the finished code version in the code download, you will notice some commented out lines. Don't worry – these don't affect the demo: they actually make it work better! Let me explain:

When writing the code for this demo, there were occasions where the desired error message wasn't appearing at the right point; it frequently ended up trapping in the very last else block at the end of the Payment Request instance. This wasn't right – in a sense it stopped because the demo didn't have BobPay installed, but the error that stopped it was not the intended one! The reason for this was it checking what the result of request. canMakePayment() was, not whether the BobPay app was installed.

As a result, the code needed to be changed slightly, hence the commented out lines (on 114, 135, and 136)! This has been done in the nobob demo in the code download, so that you can compare the changes with the printed text version. The takeaway here is that given how we've had to use several nested if statements, it pays to be very careful about how you trap for errors, and that you trap for specific errors at the right point in your code.

I know this goes without saying, but it's particularly true for the Payment Request API: there is a possibility you might trap for the wrong error, or that the wrong message is displayed, even though you've allowed for it in your error checking. Our example duplicates much of the code needed, but this is purely to show you the difference between the two versions; going forward I would look to create one version that contains error checking for both and make sure that it responds accordingly during testing.

Taking Care of Pending Transactions

We're almost at the end of this chapter, but before we take a look at our final topic, there is one more thing we should cover off briefly: pending transactions. Before you get worried, don't fret: I'm not referring to payments that have been marked as suspicious or fraudulent and should be marked as pending – no, it's something much simpler! Let me explain:

In some cases, you may want to mark an entry in the Payment Request API as pending, if it is still possible that the total price may change depending on the selections made. A good example of this might be sales tax, particularly if the customer has yet to choose their preferred delivery method.

It's easy to set in code – to do this, simply add in the pending attribute, as indicated in this code extract:

```
}, {
  label: 'Sales Tax',
  pending: true,
  amount: { currency: 'USD', value: tax.toFixed(2) }
}],
```

...yes, it's that easy, it hardly warrants a demo! The downside though is that you won't see any difference in some browsers, particularly Chrome for Windows – it will look to all intents as if nothing has changed. The only environment you may see it show something different is Chrome for Android, where it is in a shade of lighter grey, as indicated in Figure 5-13.

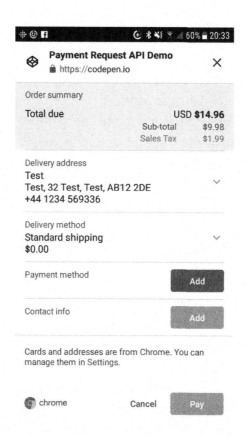

Figure 5-13. *A pending transaction*

When researching for this book, I've seen comments online that suggest it may end up being confusing for the customer to see this, as it means they are not sure what the final total will be!

This would be enough to put anyone off – it makes better sense to simply ensure that totals update every time a customer selects a different payment method or shipping option in your cart, so that when they check out, they can be confident in knowing the price displayed will be the final price they pay during checkout.

Summary

Integrating a payment method or provider into the Payment Request API is where things really start to come together – we can select the various settings we want in the checkout, before going through a payment process and end up with what we hope will be a successful transaction. We've covered a fair few tips throughout this chapter to help with the latter, so let's take a moment to review what we've learnt over the last few pages.

We kicked off with a look at the different types of integration we can use, and how they might work with the API; we then covered some of the questions we might ask about whether our integration makes use of a PSP or traditional service provider to process our payments. Next up we then got stuck into how we might implement a provider, using Stripe as our example; we began first by exploring BobPay, before walking through a theoretical example of how Stripe's system works with the API.

We then moved onto cover some key concepts that might affect payments – the first was to deal with extra charges such as for using particular payment methods, then we switched to what to do if payment apps have not been installed, and how our code structure might affect the checking process, if we've not architected our code to the best possible effect.

Now that we've come to the end of the development and theory part of this book, it's time to get really practical! In the next chapter, we're going to pull in everything we've learned and turn it into a practical example that we will run in different browsers. There will be lots to cover, so buckle up and hold on tight, as we get stuck in our next project!

CHAPTER 6

Pulling It All Together

The combined revenue of the top three ranking web sites was $113 billion in 2018, yet the average online conversion rate for desktop users is just 3%.

Remember this little icebreaker at the start of Chapter 1? It's a sobering thought that three web sites earn so much revenue between them – yes, there are a host of reasons why, but I will lay good odds that a part of the problem is our humble friend, the checkout form!

Over the course of this book, we've explored the basics of how we might configure and use the upcoming standard that is the Payment Request API. We've seen how easy it is to implement, and that making use of it will rapidly speed up the checkout process for customers, keeping them engaged and ultimately increasing conversion. There is one small problem though: although we've covered some useful techniques, many of them have been in isolation. This isn't ideal, as it means you don't get to see the full end to end process in operation, and how one small change might have a bearing on the whole setup.

Thankfully we can rectify this small omission – over the course of this chapter, we're going to bring together many of the tricks we've seen thus far and create a more end to end solution that incorporates them into the basis of a workable design. Granted, it won't be a final polished article, but it will at least give you an idea of how something might work! Without further ado, let's dive in and set the scene for what will be our project throughout this chapter.

Outlining the Project

I am sure that by now, you will have noticed a common theme in many of the projects we've worked on – yes, it goes without saying that I do have something of an affinity to coffee! It's my go-to drink when spending long hours writing code – give me a plate of (decent!) cookies, plenty of coffee, and good music, and it will keep me happy for hours…

© Alex Libby 2019
A. Libby, *Checking Out with the Payment Request API*, https://doi.org/10.1007/978-1-4842-5184-3_6

Leaving aside the wistful thinking, we're going to revisit that theme again for one more time; on this occasion, we're going to completely reskin the design. We will also add in most of the features that we've created thus far, and as a bonus, we'll also see how we can even use a preprocessor to build much of our CSS for us. At the very end of the chapter, we'll also explore one or two ideas about how we might be able to take things even further; they are not directly related to the Payment Request API, but with a little lateral thinking, anything is possible.

Okay – let's make a start: to give you a flavor of what we're creating, a screenshot of the product gallery and cart is shown in Figure 6-1.

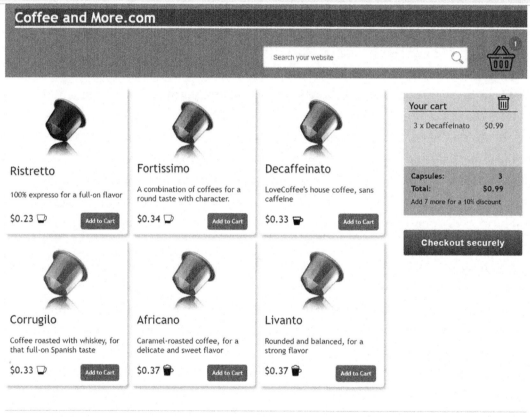

Figure 6-1. *The finished article*

Looks somewhat different to our previous design, right? For this project (and to keep things simple), we're going to forgo mobile for now; it means we can make better use of the available space on the page. There are a few other changes we've made – we have a lot to cover, so let's begin with setting up the markup and styling for our demo.

Building the Product Gallery

The first step in our project is to lay down the markup and styling for our e-commerce demo – for this, we will use a reworked version of the coffee demo we've covered a few times throughout this book.

There is one additional change we will make in this project – so far, we've used standard CSS to style the demos we've worked on thus far in this book. For this project, we're going to change this, and add in the services of a preprocessor to precompile our CSS styling.

For those of you who have yet to make use of CSS preprocessors, they use the power of JavaScript to precompile rules into valid CSS; we can use features such as basic addition, placeholder substitution, and the like to help make our CSS development more efficient.

If you are interested in learning more about Sass, then I would refer you to my book Introducing Dart Sass, published by Apress.

It's important to note though that using Sass is absolutely not obligatory – if you prefer to use plain CSS, then a version that hasn't been compiled from Sass is also available in the code download that accompanies this book. Okay – enough chitchat: let's make a start on the demo!

```
SET UP PAGE
```

For the purposes of this demo I will assume Windows, but please alter the instructions accordingly if you use a Mac- or Linux-based machine. I'm also assuming you've installed Node. js (or already have it present) and the local web server we've used thus far in the book too.

A word of note   We'll be using the command-line version of Dart Sass for this exercise; if you prefer to install via NPM, this is fine. You can find instructions on how, on the Sass web site at `https://sass-lang.com/install`.

With these in place, let's make a start:

1. We'll begin by extracting a copy of the `coffee` folder from the code download that accompanies this book; go ahead and save it at the root of our project folder.

2. Next, we need to download a copy of Sass – for this, browse to `https://github.com/sass/dart-sass/releases/` and click the link for the appropriate version for your platform.

3. Go ahead and extract the `dart-sass` folder from within this archive file, and save it within the `css` subfolder for this demo.

4. We now need to add a reference for Sass to our PC's PATH environment variable – if you are unsure on how to do this, then head over to `https://katiek2.github.io/path-doc/` for a good step-by-step tutorial for Windows, Mac, and Linux.

5. Next, fire up a Node.js terminal session, then navigate to the Dart Sass folder you saved in step 3 – on Windows it will look something like this:

    ```
    <drive>:\payment\coffee\css\dart-sass
    ```

6. At the command prompt, enter the following:

    ```
    sass C:\payment\coffee\css\styles-sass.scss c:\payment\coffee\css\styles.css
    ```

The format for compiling Sass is sass <path to source file> <path to destination file> – please alter the locations accordingly, if you are using something different. Notice though that I've deliberately set different folders; the results will compile straight into the `css` folder by default.

---

7. Navigate back to the `coffee` folder, then at the prompt, enter `ws --hostname localhost --https` and press Enter.

8. You will see a URL for our local web server – enter this into Chrome, to view the results thus far for our demo.

At this point, we will have a basic product gallery in place, where we can select products and drop them into our basket. The markup we've used to create the gallery area is standard HTML; it's worth taking a look at both this and the script used to populate the gallery and operate the cart, in more detail.

Dissecting the Code thus Far

If we take a look in more detail at the markup we've used, we should begin to see some familiar code in place – elements such as the `#message <div>` have been lifted from previous demos elsewhere in the book.

We begin by defining our main #container element, which hosts the whole page – this contains the `<header>` element which displays the title, product count, and shopping basket icon.

Next up comes a rather substantial block for the search box – it's somewhat ironic that the largest block in the markup is actually the one block that is only there for presentation and doesn't even operate! The set of numbers in the `<path...>` element at line 22 relates to the magnifying glass icon, which is an SVG icon; we could have used a standard JPEG or PNG image instead, but SVG icons can be hosted inline which reduces the need for the server to have to shell out for another resource.

If we skip past line 41 for a moment, the next block is the shopping cart itself; it contains an empty unordered list as the placeholder element, ready for populating with products we've selected from the gallery. Next up comes the total box, which will display the total cost before shipping, sales tax, and any additional charges or discounts; below this is the Checkout securely button.

We then finish with the extra information area which we've lifted from the extra info demo back in Chapter 3; this simulates an opportunity for customers to give extra instructions, such as which button to press if the customer lived in a shared block of apartments.

Making Our Gallery Work

In our quick run through of the markup, you will have noticed that we've skipped past line 41. There is a good reason for this – that empty placeholder `<div>` is used to populate our shopping demo with products, which we do making use of the code in scripts.js.

Let's open this file up in a text editor and take a look at it in more detail – it kicks off by creating a series of variables and two object arrays; the latter to store the product details and keep tally of the products we drop into the basket.

Moving on, we then have the generateProductList function at line 67 – this is used to populate the products <div> from our markup with the items in our store. Within this function, we create a list item for each product dropped into the cart; this contains the item.quantity and item.product.name values, along with the subtotal for that product and total number of capsules ordered.

The remainder of the code in this function takes care of adding a discount – we first divide the capsule count by 10, using the mod operator. If this gives 0 as a result, then we know we've hit a value where we can apply the discount. If, however, the value is not zero, we subtract the remainder from 10, to give us the total left that the customer must add before they qualify for the discount. You might though wonder why the discount amount is updated using a setTimeout() value, right? There is a good reason for this: it allows the code time to update the total amount when more products are added; doing it sooner and the discount value will be overridden by the next update of the cart.

The next function in the scripts.js file is generateCartButtons – this takes care of making various elements in the cart visible when products have been added. This is purely for usability purposes only: we don't want people to try to check out with an empty cart! We then finish out with setting up some event handlers to take care of updating the cart (or productsInCart array), before setting up an init function to initiate the creation of our product list and event handlers.

Setting Up the Basic Basket

With the basic UI in place, we can now turn our attention to making it work – we already have the requisite code in place to populate our product gallery and add items into the basket; this is taken care of by scripts.js within the scripts folder. The next stage is to add in the code that will initiate an instance of the Payment Request API as our checkout form – we'll begin by setting up a basic instance of our basket, before adding functionality to it over the course of this chapter.

SETTING UP THE BASIC BASKET

Our first task is to set up the basic basket, so let's make a start:

1. We'll begin by opening a new file in your text editor – save this as `payment.js` in the `js` subfolder under the coffee folder.

2. Next, go ahead and the following lines in, to initiate a call to the Payment Request API, as soon as the page has loaded:

```
window.onload = function(e) {
...enter code here...
}
```

3. We first need to add in a constant value to define our supported payment methods – for this, add in the following lines inside the `window.onload` block, starting at line 2:

```
const paymentMethods = [{
  supportedMethods: 'basic-card',
    data: {
      supportedNetworks: ['visa', 'mastercard', 'amex']
    }
}];
```

4. The next step is to add in an event handler that will be fired in response to clicks on the Checkout securely button – this is where the bulk of the work takes place. For this, add in the following placeholder, leaving a blank line under the function from the previous step:

```
document.querySelector(".chkoutbutton").addEventListener("click",
function(e) {
  if (document.querySelector(".chkoutbutton").classList
  .contains("enabled")) {
  document.getElementById("message").className = ";

  ...enter code here...
  }
});
```

5. We now come to the crux of our demo – the Payment Request API call.
    We first need to check that our browser can support it, so add this in after the
    `document.getElementById("message")`...line of code from the previous
    step, leaving a blank line in-between:

```
if (window.PaymentRequest) {
...enter code here...
}
```

6. We now have to define a number of variables – these will take care of the
    relevant values passed to the API, such as shipping, sales tax, and total. Add the
    code below, inside the `window.PaymentRequest` condition:

```
let subtotal = Number(document.querySelector(".total-price").
innerText);
let shipping = 2.99;
let tax = (subtotal + shipping) * 0.175;
let total = Number(subtotal) + Number(tax) + Number(shipping);
```

7. Next up comes the `paymentDetails` block – this will manage the various
    labels and values that we display when the checkout form is rendered on
    screen:

```
const paymentDetails = {
  total: {
    label: 'Total to pay by card',
    amount: { currency: 'USD', value:  total.toFixed(2) }
  },
    displayItems: [{
    label: 'Coffee capsules',
    amount: { currency: 'USD', value: subtotal.toFixed(2) }
  }, {
    label: 'Sales Tax',
    amount: { currency: 'USD', value: tax.toFixed(2) }
  }],
};
```

8. We have two more variables to declare – these set the information that should be displayed or requested in the checkout form, as well as initiate an instance of the Payment Request API. Add these below the variables from the previous step, leaving a blank line in-between:

```
const paymentOptions = { requestPayerEmail: true };
let request = new PaymentRequest(paymentMethods, paymentDetails,
paymentOptions);
```

9. We're almost done – the final block takes care of managing the response from the server and determining what to display; for the purposes of this demo, we are simulating the response, but this is where we will get notification from our PSP as to whether the transaction has been successful or has failed. Add this block in below the previous two declarations, leaving a blank line in-between:

```
if (request.canMakePayment) {
  request.canMakePayment().then(function(result) {
    if (result) {
      request.show().then(function(result) {
        result.complete('success').then(function() {
          console.log(JSON.stringify(result));
        });
      }).catch(function(err) {
        console.error(err.message);
      });
    } else {
      console.log('Cannot make payment');
    }
  }).catch(function(err) {
    console.log(request, err);
  });
}
```

10. At this point we're done with editing – go ahead and save your work. It's time now to preview the results of our efforts – for this, fire up a Node.js terminal session, then navigate to the `coffee` folder we created back in step 1.

11.   At the prompt, enter this command and press Enter:

```
ws --hostname localhost --https
```

Go ahead and browse to `https://localhost:8000` when prompted – if all is well, we should see our checkout form appear once we've added some test products and hit the Checkout securely button. The form will look something similar to the screenshot shown in Figure 6-2.

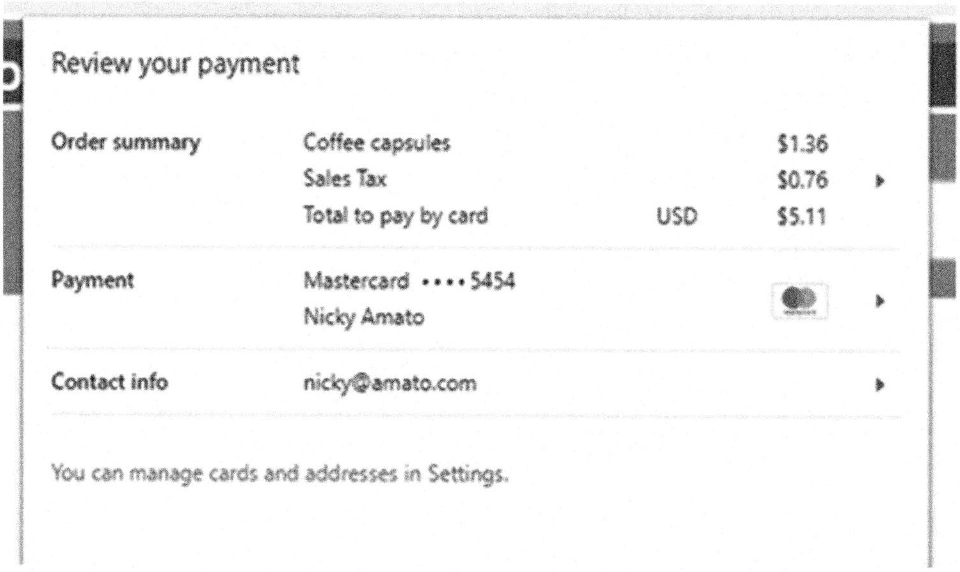

Figure 6-2. *The completed base checkout form*

Hopefully that wasn't too difficult – we're using the same principles first introduced back in Chapter 2; nothing should be too unfamiliar! If, however you get stuck, there is an example of how it should look in the Examples folder, in the code download that accompanies this book.

Assuming all is well, we've revisited some key techniques that we first saw earlier in the book – let's take a moment to remind ourselves of the key parts to a basic checkout form created using the API, before we continue with adding more functionality to our project.

Breaking Apart the Code

When creating a checkout form, we have to include at least four different components, alongside the event handler that will fire up our instance of the API – these are payment methods, payment details, and payment options. At this point I should make it clear though that we're not talking about components in the sense of a framework such as React but more blocks of code that need to be incorporated for a basic checkout form!

With this in mind, if we take a look at the payment.js file we've just created, we start with defining a const value to store the supported payment methods, which we call paymentMethods. The bulk of the code is then stored in the event handler that is fired when clicking on the Checkout securely button – this is parsed only if we can satisfy the initial check that confirms our Checkout securely button is enabled.

We then define a number of variables to store values for subtotal, shipping tax, and the final total. We've stored these within the window.PaymentRequest object; otherwise they become inaccessible when rendering the form (you can see them on or around lines 57-60). Next up, we defined our paymentDetails block, which details what labels and values should be displayed, before building up the final options that are used to initiate our instance of the Payment Request API.

The real magic happens in the final condition check – here we determine if we have at least one payment method available (request.canMakePayment); if so, we go through the steps of displaying the form and determining if the response back results in a successful or failed transaction for our customer.

Note   For the purposes of this demo, we will simulate a positive or negative response almost immediately; in reality this is likely to take a little longer as we would shell out to the PSP at this point in the process.

Taking Care of Shipping (Plus Restrictions)

We now have a basic checkout form in place, where we can see details such as the total cost of the purchase, available methods of payment, and the like. This is a good start but, as we've already seen earlier in this book, is only part of the story!

At this stage, we can now begin to add in the code that will take care of the missing features, such as updating shipping options, selecting a PSP, and so on. The first of these options that we will add in is shipping; for this, we'll begin by setting the form to show the shipping address, so that our checkout process knows to where we'll be shipping the selected products.

CONFIGURING SHIPPING AND RELATED EXCLUSIONS

We have a fair bit of code to add in for this next demo, so let's crack on:

1. All of the code we need to add will sit in the `payment.js` file, so if you don't already have it open, please revert back to it.

2. The first change we need to make is to add in a shipping entry to our `paymentDetails` block; this goes in immediately after the `displayItems` configuration option, as highlighted in the following:

```
displayItems: [{
  label: 'Coffee capsules',
  amount: { currency: 'USD', value: subtotal.toFixed(2) }
}, {
  label: 'Standard shipping in US',
  amount: { currency: 'USD', value: shipping.toFixed(2) }
}, {
```

3. Next, we need to tell our instance of the Payment Request API that we now want to ask for shipping details; add in the `requestShipping` parameter as indicated:

```
const paymentOptions = {
  requestPayerEmail: true,
  requestShipping: true,
};
```

4. Now that we've set up the API to request shipping details, we need to tell it how to handle any changes; this is the responsibility of two handlers – the first, `shippingaddresschange`, responds to any changes in the chosen address. Leave a line after the two variables we declared in the previous step, then add in this event handler:

```
request.addEventListener('shippingaddresschange', function(evt) {
  evt.updateWith(new Promise(function(resolve) {
    updateDetails(paymentDetails, request.shippingAddress, resolve,
    total);
  }));
});
```

5. The second handler, `shippingaddressoptions`, fires if we need to adjust the shipping costs based on the selected address. Go ahead and add in this code below the `shippingaddresschange` event handler:

```
request.addEventListener('shippingoptionchange', function(evt) {
  evt.updateWith(new Promise(function(resolve, reject) {
    updateDetails(paymentDetails, request.shippingOption,
    resolve, reject, total);
  }));
});
```

This is only part of the story though – while we may not need to initiate any changes based on altering the selected address, we will likely need to if the new address qualifies for a change in shipping costs:

6. The previous step refers to an `updateDetails` function; go ahead and add in this block of code after the paymentMethods constant at the top of the file. It's a substantial function, so we'll break it down into sections, starting with an initial declaration for `shippingOption`:

```
function updateDetails(details, shippingAddress, callback, stotal) {
  let shippingOption = {
    id: ",
    label: ",
    amount: {currency: 'USD', value: '0.00'},
    selected: true,
    pending: false,
  };
```

7. This next block determines where the target address is and swaps over the shipping options based on where it is in the United States or indicates that we can't ship to destinations outside of the United States:

```
if (shippingAddress.country === 'US') {
  if (shippingAddress.region === 'CA') {
    shippingOption.id = 'californiaFreeShipping';
    shippingOption.label = 'Free shipping in California';
    details.total.amount.value = (Number(stotal)).toFixed(2);
  } else {
    shippingOption.id = 'unitedStatesStandardShipping';
    shippingOption.label = 'Standard shipping in US';
    shippingOption.amount.value = '2.99';
    details.total.amount.value = (Number(stotal) + Number(3.99)).
      toFixed(2);
  }
  details.shippingOptions = [shippingOption];
  delete details.error;
} else {
  // Don't ship outside of US for the purposes of this example.
  shippingOption.label = 'Shipping';
  shippingOption.pending = true;
  details.total.amount.value = (Number(stotal)).toFixed(2);
  details.error = 'Sorry - cannot ship outside of USA.';
  delete details.shippingOptions;
}
details.displayItems.splice(1, 1, shippingOption);
callback(details);
}
```

8. We have a couple more changes to make to incorporate shipping into our instance of the Payment Request API: the first is to add in the options that should be displayed to the user, based on the selected address. For this, look for the closing comma at the end of the Sales Tax option, and add in the following code as indicated:

```
label: 'Sales Tax',
amount: { currency: 'USD', value: tax.toFixed(2) }
}], shippingOptions: [{
```

```
id: 'standard',
label: 'Standard shipping in US',
amount: {currency: 'USD', value: shipping.toFixed(2)},
selected: true,
},
{
id: 'express',
label: 'Express delivery (next day)',
amount: {currency: 'USD', value: '3.99'},
},
],
```

9. We're almost there – the next change is to add in a default error clause that will kick in if we choose an address that is not supported. Add this line in below the closing], from the previous step:

```
error: "Sorry - we can't deliver to that address.",
shippingOptions: [],
```

10. The last change we need to make is to add in an extra text box – this is displayed at the end of a successful transaction, to invite the customer to leave any additional instructions for delivery. Add these statements in after the displayMessage(...) entry inside result.complete (on or around line 123), within the request.show() block:

```
const additionalDetailsContainer = document
.getElementById('instructions');
additionalDetailsContainer.style.display = 'block';
additionalDetailsContainer.focus();
```

11. All of the changes are now complete for this stage – go ahead and save your work. We can now preview the results of our efforts: for this, fire up a Node.js terminal session, then navigate to the coffee folder we created back in step 1.

12. At the prompt, enter this command and press Enter:

```
ws --hostname localhost --https
```

13. Go ahead and browse to `https://localhost:8000` when prompted – if all is well, we should see our checkout form appear once we've added some test products and hit the Checkout securely button. The form will look something similar to the screenshot shown in Figure 6-3.

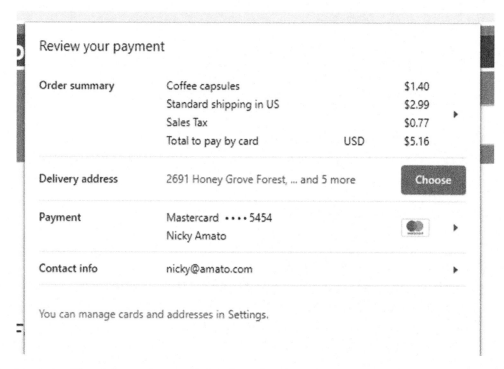

Figure 6-3. *The shipping option displayed, when displaying the form for the first time*

14. Try hitting the Choose button – if you don't already have one, go ahead and add in an address that is based outside of the United States. The exact details do not matter, as long as it is not based in the States. What happens if you then try to select it? You will see the error displayed in Figure 6-4.

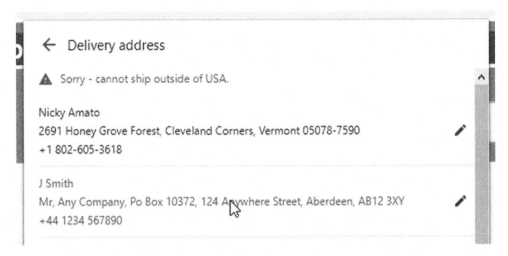

Figure 6-4. *What happens when we select a not-supported address…*

Phew – that was some demo! It may have seemed a lot of code, but how we handle shipping is critical to the success of any transaction. We've already seen much of this code from earlier demos, but nevertheless it is worth us taking a moment to review it in detail, while we have a pause before tackling the next exercise.

Exploring the Code in More Detail

We first met shipping as a featured part of the API, way back in Chapter 4 – we explored how we had to add in something to cover both changes to the address and to the chosen option when displaying the checkout form.

There is nothing new this time around – it might seem like we've added a fair amount of code, but in reality, this is likely to be par for the norm when it comes to configuring shipping! We kicked off with adding in the necessary `label` and `amount` in the checkout form, before specifying the `requestShipping` parameter as part of the payment options.

Next up, we then added in two event handlers: the first took care of managing changes to addresses. In most cases, this doesn't need to fire any callback event in itself; we just need the form to render the new address. The second (`shippingaddressoptions`) however is more important: it fires a request to the `updateDetails` function to determine if we are shipping to a supported location and whether we need to update both the shipping cost and total amount as a result of changing the address. In both cases, we use the `shippingOption` variable to store the updated values, before splicing them back into our original checkout form.

The final changes we made were to specify the details that should be shown, depending (in this example) on whether we were shipping to an address based in California, the rest of the United States, or elsewhere. For the former, we set free shipping; for the rest of the United States, we specify standard shipping, and anything else is marked as not being available for selection.

Handling Payments

We're making steady process on our form – at this stage we have our basic shop front in place, with an initial checkout form being displayed when we hit the Checkout securely button. We've added in code to take care of updating the shipping options, so we now know where to ship the products; it's time to sort out payments!

For these next few exercises, we're going to build on the `basic-card` option that we've already included in the initial setup earlier in this chapter. We'll begin with adding in a third-party payment method in the form of BobPay, before taking care of displaying discounts or applying extra charges when needed during checkout.

Integrating a Payment Method

There are dozens of different payment providers that we can hook into when accepting payments – although we can choose to go directly with the likes of Google Pay or Amazon Pay, it makes better sense to hook in the services of a PSP such as Stripe. They can take care of supporting multiple providers, providing access via a single unified setup.

Unfortunately, as we touched on earlier in this book, we can't use the likes of Stripe: instead, we will make use of BobPay to simulate how integrating a payment method will work. We're going to use code we've already created from earlier – let's make a start on adding it into our project.

INTEGRATING A PAYMENT METHOD

We only have a couple of changes that need to be made – the first is to install BobPay:

If, when you browse to the BobPay web site, you see "Uninstall BobPay Web Payment App," please skip to step 2.

---

1. We'll start by browsing to `https://bobpay.xyz` – scroll down to the bottom of the page and click the link marked "Install BobPay Web Payment App." The link will change the link to "Uninstall BobPay Web Payment App," when complete.

2. Next, revert back to the `payment.js` file we had open from the previous demo – look for the closing comma on line 7, then add in the following code:

```
, {
    supportedMethods: 'https://bobpay.xyz/pay'
}, {
    supportedMethods: 'interledger'
}
```

3. All of the changes are now complete for this stage – go ahead and save your work. We can now preview the results of our efforts: for this, fire up a Node.js terminal session, then navigate to the `coffee` folder we created back in step 1.

4. At the prompt, enter this command and press Enter:

```
ws --hostname localhost --https
```

5. Go ahead and browse to `https://localhost:8000` when prompted – if all is well, we should see our checkout form appear once we've added some test products and hit the Checkout securely button. The form will look something similar to the screenshot shown in Figure 6-5, where we see the tree icon signifying BobPay:

	Sales Tax		$0.78
	Total to pay by card	USD	$5.22
Payment	Pay with BobPay		
	bobpay.xyz		
Contact info	nicky@amato.com		

Figure 6-5. *Confirmation that BobPay is installed...*

Unlike other exercises in this chapter, this one was significantly easier to complete, chuckle! It's worth noting though that in production, we will have more work to do; we'll revisit this shortly, once we've quickly reviewed the code we've inserted into our demo.

Exploring the Code in More Detail

One of the challenges we face when working with the Payment Request API is testing payment methods. Granted, if we decided to use the services of a PSP, then we can make use of their test environment before publishing our site. We would absolutely do this, but what about testing to make sure that our site actually works, before committing to a PSP?

This is where BobPay kicks in – it's perfect for simulating what would happen when we use a payment method such as Google Pay or Apple Pay. In this demo, we began with enabling it for our site – as with any third-party payment method, we have to make sure it is available on our site, before customers can use it to purchase products.

We then updated the `paymentMethods` constant to include the BobPay option, so that our checkout form now knows to offer it; as a bonus, it included a link to the Interledger payment method too, which we touched on back in Chapter 5.

Okay – let's change tack and move on: we have a couple more areas to cover that can affect the total amounts we pass through to the API. One of these we already covered when we created our initial markup: hands up anyone who **hasn't** tried to find a discount or promo code when purchasing something online?

Displaying Discounts

Any one shopping online will want to find the best price, or get the best discount they can – retailers operating online should have lower cost base than brick-and-mortar outfits and so can offer products at reduced prices. Indeed, I've heard of countless stories over the years, where we might go into a brick-and-mortar outfit to window shop, only to then go online to purchase the same product at a reduced price! It's tough for brick-and-mortar outfits, but hey – that's life….

I digress: time to fall back to reality. If we take a look back at the beginning of this chapter, you will see that we've actually already added in the code for a simple 10% off the total price when purchasing capsules in blocks of ten.

I can see the next question coming though – how come we've not implemented this as part of the Payment Request API? There is a good reason for this: we only need to provide it with the final total price. As we've already seen, space is a little limited when it comes to adding in the various labels – the simplest option is to do the math in the basket, then pass in the final result to the API. In this instance, we would pass through $1.45 if we were to hit the Checkout Securely button shown in Figure 6-6.

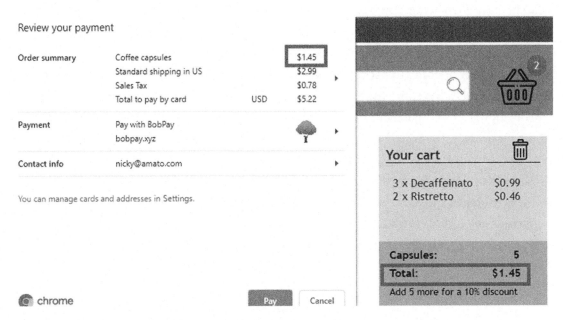

Figure 6-6. *Passing the discounted value to the API*

There is a downside to the approach we've used: how can we tell if the price we've passed has indeed been discounted? Yes, this does seem somewhat ironic that I've recommended doing the heavy lifting in the basket, yet I still don't follow my own advice!

It does go to show though that we need to be super clear about what is presented to the customer. Here, we could put an indication that the price is discounted or perhaps adjust the message to show how many selected capsules qualify for the discount. These is absolutely something we need to consider when designing the overall user experience for our project, so that we pass the right value through and give customers confidence in the values displayed on screen.

Applying Charges When Necessary

There comes a point where a retailer might have to apply an additional charge – this should be to cover additional costs that can't be absorbed elsewhere.

However, this has been subject to some abuse over the years, with some charging vastly inflated charges that don't really represent the true cost incurred, perhaps seen as a deterrent to customers, so retailers can avoid the paperwork involved. This came to a head in early 2018, where the EU Payment Services Directive (PSD2) has banned the use of surcharges on all debit or credit cards within the EU.

It means that using this option can put you on shaky grounds; you will need a very good reason for needing to use it that doesn't contravene this directive if dealing with EU companies! At the same time, research has also indicated that there have been consistency issues with earlier versions of the API and how charges were being applied. At the moment, it seems to be a case of these only working when using third-party providers and **not** the basic-card option; it is possible that this might change once the API becomes a mainstream standard.

This aside, let's take a look at the mechanics of how this will work in our project – we've touched on this from earlier in the book, but this time around we'll make some improvements to how the code operates.

APPLYING CHARGES WHERE NEEDED

---

1. We'll begin by opening a copy of the payment.js file from within the coffee folder we've been working with throughout this chapter – we only need to make a single change within this file.

2. Look for the closing bracket, brace, and comma after the 'Sales Tax' entry – enter the following code immediately afterward on the next line:

```
modifiers: [{
  supportedMethods: 'https://bobpay.xyz/pay',
    additionalDisplayItems: [{
      label: 'Processing fee',
      amount: { currency: 'USD', value: '3.00' }
    }],
    total: {
      label: 'Total to pay by BobPay',
      amount: {currency: 'USD', value: Number(total + 3).toFixed(2)}}
  }],
```

3. Go ahead and save your work.

At this point we need to make sure BobPay is installed – if you don't already have it set up, then go back to the previous exercise and complete steps 1 and 2 before continuing:

1. It's time to preview our work, so fire up a Node.js terminal session, then navigate to the coffee folder we created at the beginning of this chapter. At the prompt, enter this command and press Enter:

```
ws --hostname localhost --https
```

2. Go ahead and browse to https://localhost:8000 when prompted – if all is well, we should see our checkout form appear once we've added some test products and hit the Checkout securely button. The form will look something similar to the screenshot shown in Figure 6-7, where we can see the two more items entry appear, along with BobPay set as the default Payment method.

173

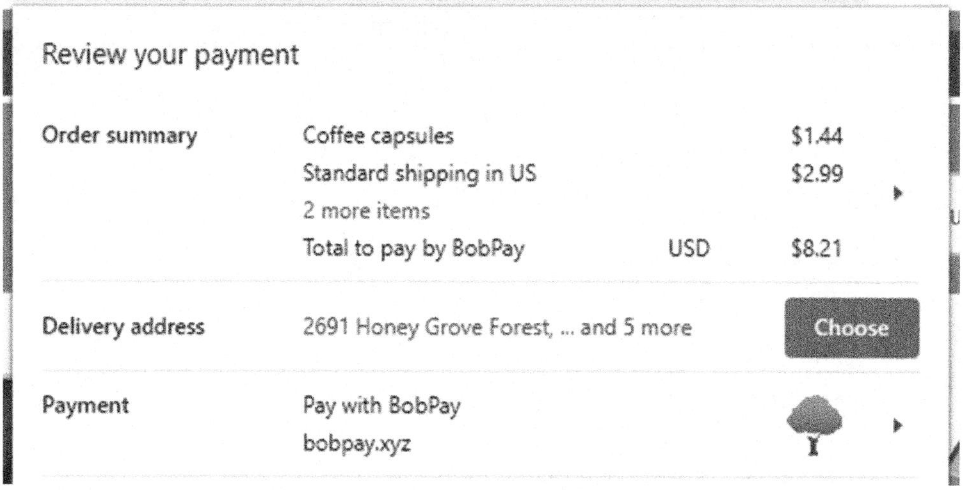

Review your payment

Order summary	Coffee capsules		$1.44
	Standard shipping in US		$2.99
	2 more items		
	Total to pay by BobPay	USD	$8.21
Delivery address	2691 Honey Grove Forest, ... and 5 more		Choose
Payment	Pay with BobPay		
	bobpay.xyz		

Figure 6-7. *The initial display, when adding supplementary charges...*

3. Try clicking the arrow to the right of Order summary. We should see a processing fee entry for $3.00 appear, and the total label text has changed to confirm we're paying by BobPay, as illustrated in Figure 6-8.

Sales Tax		$0.78
Processing fee		$3.00
Total to pay by BobPay	USD	$8.21

Figure 6-8. *Confirmation of the extra charge being applied*

4. If we revert back to the payment review window and select a different card, the screen will automatically update – this time the two extra items entry will not be present as we're using an alternative means of payment (Figure 6-9).

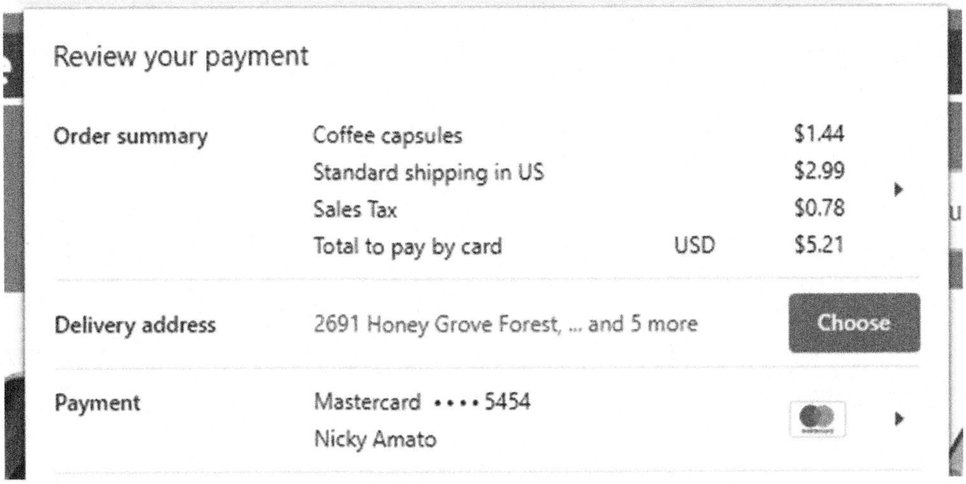

Figure 6-9. *No supplementary charges being added*

At face value, this is a very simple change to make – it opens up a route for us to pass on additional costs to the customer, should the need arise. There is a downside to this though; customers (quite rightly) will get annoyed if we're adding costs at this late stage! When we first covered this back in Chapter 5, we touched on a very important point about this – it's worth revisiting this again as we review the code we've just added in more detail.

Exploring the Code in More Detail

The code we've added for this demo is very straightforward – we kick off by adding the modifiers configuration option, which takes two parameters: `supportedMethods` and `additionalDisplayItems`. For the first, we specify the methods which are supported for the modifier and thus are the ones where extra charges should be applied (in this case, the URL for BobPay):

```
modifiers: [{
  supportedMethods: 'https://bobpay.xyz/pay',
```

For the second, we need to specify both the label and new amount; note that this is just for the charge and not the new total (that comes shortly):

```
additionalDisplayItems: [{
  label: 'Processing fee',
  amount: { currency: 'USD', value: '3.00' }
}],
```

The final section requires us to update the total label and new amount – this needs to include the extra charge which we have to add manually, as the API will not calculate this for us automatically:

```
total: {
  label: 'Total to pay by BobPay',
  amount: {currency: 'USD', value: Number(total + 3).toFixed(2)}
  }
}],
```

The API takes care of updating the view automatically for us, when switching between payment methods; as long as the supported payment types match the existing name, it will update automatically.

Applying Charges: A Postscript

At face value this seems to work very well – we can pass on costs to customers if needed, so there is no pressure to have to absorb costs and therefore inflate prices any further than is necessary....right?

Wrong – all is not as peachy as it might first seem! When we first explored the application of extra charges, we touched on a very important point: adding extra charges at this late stage is more likely to annoy and infuriate customers than keep them happy. Let me explain:

Customers by their very nature do not like extra charges being applied without warning – it affects the level of confidence they have in our site, as they begin to think that if we have one extra charge, is what they see *really* the final price? It is understandable – after all, how would you feel if you suddenly had to pay out for extra charges you didn't anticipate having to pay?

I would absolutely advise using this option with care – I've provided it purely as a technical demonstration of what is possible. I've seen indications that modifiers have had something of a checkered history: they currently only work for third-party payment methods and not the basic-card option we've used throughout many of the demos in this book. This doesn't mean to say that we shouldn't use it – far from it: I would just make sure that you absolutely have to use it and that there isn't an alternative that would be safer and likely to instill more confidence for customers to your site.

Adding Error Handling

So far, we've put together a workable instance of the Payment Request API, which allows us to select a preferred method of payment, choose the right delivery address (or add on), and of course display a high-level summary of our order.

The trouble is, and with the best will in the world, there will always be occasions where things don't quite go according to plan! Mistakes can, and do, happen – we might enter invalid details, or even worse our card or payment method may be declined. The way we handle this will depend largely on whether we use the basic-card method or a PSP; this said, we can at least provide some basic error checking to get us started.

There are a few places where we can add in some form of error management – at a minimum, we should put in a slot to display error messages; we can also put in something to manage cancellation of the form, confirm that no valid payment methods exist, or if indeed there's been a problem with payment. We've already seen how to add these in isolation, so without further ado, let's put them into our project, so that we can see them in action as part of a bigger solution.

TAKING CARE OF ERRORS

All of the changes we need to make will be in the payments.js file, so make sure you have this open first, before continuing with these steps:

1. Add a blank line after the `paymentMethods` constant, then on the next line, add in this function, which will take care of rendering the message on screen for us:

```
function displayMessage(symbol, state, mesg) {
  document.getElementById("message").classList.add(state);
  document.getElementById("message").innerHTML = "<span>" + symbol +
  "</span>" + mesg;
}
```

2. Scroll down the page to the console.log statement on or around line 122; immediately after it, add in this line of code:

```
displayMessage("\u2714", "success", "Payment received - thanks for
your order!");
```

3. We have two catch blocks within our code – the first takes care of any errors or issues, assuming that we at least have been able to attempt payment. Replace the contents of the catch() block as indicated:

```
}).catch(function(err) {
  if (err.code == DOMException.ABORT_ERR) {
    displayMessage("&#128712;", "info", "Request has been cancelled");
  } else {
    console.error(err.message);
    displayMessage("\u2716", "error", "There was a problem with
    payment");
  }
});
} else {
  console.log('Cannot make payment');
  displayMessage("&#128712;", "info", "Sorry - no valid payment
  methods available");
}
```

4. We're done with editing – go ahead and save your work. Next, we can now preview the results of our change – for this, fire up a Node.js terminal session, then navigate to the coffee folder we created at the beginning of this chapter.

5. At the prompt, enter this command and press Enter:

```
ws --hostname localhost --https
```

6. Go ahead and browse to https://localhost:8000 when prompted, then run through a test purchase; if all is well, we should see an example of our message now being displayed below the cart, as indicated in Figure 6-10.

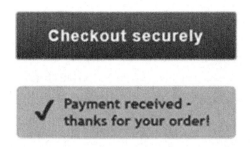

Figure 6-10. *The finished message being displayed*

There is a real irony about this change – it's probably one of the simplest we've had to do but can arguably have the most impact for our customers! It's vitally important that we add in appropriate messaging; even though this is not strictly part of the API, it is still something that we must factor into the overall checkout process. There are a couple of important points that are worth exploring in more detail, so let's quickly review the code we've added in the last exercise in more detail.

Exploring the Code in More Detail

The changes made in this exercise are very straightforward – we kicked off by adding in a generic function `displayMessage()` to render any messages we create on screen, in the message <div> below the cart on the right.

Further on down the page, in the `response.complete('success')` block, we updated the code to display a suitably-worded success message using this function. At the same time, we added in calls to display suitable messages if the request had been cancelled or if there was an issue with payment (details of which we log to the console).

It's worth noting that in this instance, we used the `DOMException` object to confirm if a request has been aborted. We could use `err.message` to achieve something similar, although this method isn't as clean! If we had, we would have had to look for an instance of "Request cancelled" in the response rather than a purely numerical value that is returned when using `DOMException`.

For more details about using DOM Exception, please refer to the article on Mozilla's Developer Network site, available at `https://developer.mozilla.org/en-US/docs/Web/API/DOMException`.

Taking Things Further

We've almost reached the end of constructing our project – while it will work perfectly fine as it is, there are still a few things we can add to help finesse the overall experience for our customers. As a minimum, we should absolutely fine-tune some of the selectors we've used – for demo purposes, we can get away with this, but in a production environment where speed is key, we should ensure our code is fully optimized.

However, there is plenty of scope to take things further in terms of functionality; to give you a flavor of what might be possible, let's take a look at a few ideas:

- Currencies – this is not supported by default in the API; we must rely on browser localization for this to work. However, we can at least perform basic currency localization, provided we store currency values as plain floating-point numbers, and define the currency symbol separately. We've touched on this in a limited capacity, but for a more robust solution, how about retrieving values from a database as soon as we decide to select a different currency? Of course, there are concerns with performance (and SEO?) if we're doing this for anything more than just a small setup; this is something we should consider if we decide to use this option.

- Adding in a payment option update – we've used event handlers to determine if changes are made to either the shipping address or option, but not to the selected payment method. Fortunately, there is one we can use if need, which is the `PaymentMethodChangeEvent` – this would need to be called if the customer decided to change to using a store card, from using something such as Apple Pay.

- Skipping the initial form – this may seem a little controversial (given this is the main topic of the book!), but it may be worth considering if skipping the initial selection options could be useful for us? One of the developers for Chromium, Rouslan Solomakhin, created a set of demos that does this – his example for Google Pay can be seen at `https://rsolomakhin.github.io/pr/wait-gp/pr.js`.

- Geolocation – most recent browsers support this protocol; how about using it to determine if you are within say a 5-mile (8 km) radius, for example? This would be perfect for food takeaway outlets, who frequently offer free delivery if you are local but charge if you fall outside of their target area.

- Adding in support for a payment method if it isn't available – we've touched on using BobPay, but this is something to consider for customers. Should we display a message to indicate it isn't installed and redirect as we did? Or should we only display buttons for those payment options that are available?

- Adding in a retry option – this is not something we've added in yet, as the API standard is still in a state of flux and that not all browsers fully support this option yet. However, I would recommend checking a site such as CanIUse.com to see if this has changed – you can see the latest picture at `https://caniuse.com/#feat=payment-request`.

Hopefully this will give you some idea of where we can go with the Payment Request API – it's a good excuse to get really creative and use other libraries or frameworks to help produce a more rounded experience for customers. The API has yet to reach a confirmed standard at the time of writing, so things may change; it is worth checking the W3C documentation on this standard, although it does make for somewhat dry reading!

The W3C documentation can be found at `https://github.com/w3c/payment-request`; I would also recommend checking the MDN wiki for the Payment Request API too, at `https://developer.mozilla.org/en-US/docs/Web/API/Payment_Request_API`.

Summary

Phew – we've reached the end of creating our complete demo! Although we've covered a lot of code, none of it should be unfamiliar by now; it's all code we've met at various stages throughout this book but brought together to show it in operation as a complete unit. Let's take a few moments to recap through what we've covered in this chapter.

We kicked off with a quick introduction to the project we would be working on in this chapter; this was swiftly followed with a look at setting up the basic markup and styling, ready for us to add in each feature. We then covered the code we would need to make the basic basket operate, before starting to add in extra features to fine-tune the experience for our customers.

The first feature added in was shipping – we covered the methods required to manage both changes to the address we choose, as well as the method of delivery. We then switched to installing the additional BobPay payment method, to simulate how tying in a payment method would work in a working example, before exploring how we might offer a simple discount for purchasing multiples of our chosen product, coffee capsules. We also touched on handling extra charges, but with a warning to confirm that this practice is frowned upon and ideally should not be used unless absolutely necessary.

The last feature we covered was a look at basic error handling – we saw that although this is not a standard part of the API, it is nevertheless an important consideration; we explored some of the various points we might need to hook in appropriate indications to our customers, based on the outcome of an action. We then rounded out the chapter by exploring some of the ideas we could look at implementing, such as geolocation, which will help improve the experience for our customers.

We've certainly covered a lot throughout this chapter, but there is one big element missing though: many developers will use frameworks such as React or Vue.js rather than code sites from scratch. What does this mean for using the Request Payment API? Do we need to change things, or will it play happily, without too much change required? Aha – stay with me on this: I will reveal more in the next chapter.

CHAPTER 7

Project: Enabling the API in a Framework or CMS

I'm going to break with convention and ask you to do something – granted, it's a little unusual, but stay with me on this: it will all become clear! If you enter "top 10 JavaScript frameworks," what do you get back?

I'll lay good odds that, at least at the time of writing, you'll see the likes of React, Vue.js, or Angular feature somewhere in that list, right? One can't help but notice that these have become really popular over the last few years, so unless you've been hiding somewhere, there's going to come a time when we have to work with at least one of these frameworks over the course of the next few years.

So – how does this fit in? Well, so far, we've worked on using the Payment Request API in a static HTML environment. This works perfectly well, and there is nothing wrong with this approach. However, I know that some of you will likely work with a framework, such as Angular, React, or Vue.js; I'll bet you're probably asking: "what does this mean for me?"

The great thing about the Payment Request API is that it can be configured to work with most of the popular frameworks out there – such as React or Angular – and that those of you who use one will of course have their personal favorite. Ignoring the use of frameworks isn't a good idea – it's time we stepped up and took a look at an example in more detail! We'll do this in the form of a mini project over the course of this chapter; this will start with a look at setting the scene for our project.

© Alex Libby 2019
A. Libby, *Checking Out with the Payment Request API*, https://doi.org/10.1007/978-1-4842-5184-3_7

Outlining the Project

As a developer and author, I spend many hours in front of my laptop, writing code or words – there are times when it feels like I become submerged, only to pop up every so often for a breath of fresh air. Okay, perhaps that's a little extreme: the two things I do like to have with me though when writing is a good mug of steaming coffee and a plate of cookies.

I should point out that we're not talking about any ol' cookies here – oh no: they have to be just right. Soft, chewy with only a thin crispy coating – yes, it's enough to make your mouth water.

But I digress – back to reality: we've already built a simple e-commerce store around coffee, so there are no prizes for guessing that our next store will be around cookies! We're going to build a simple store to select from a selection of cookies and simulate processing payments through an instance of the Payment Request API. The next question though is: what framework are we going to use?

Exploring the Options

Throughout the course of this book, the emphasis has been on creating static HTML-based content, to serve as our product store. There is nothing wrong in this approach – indeed, this will help SEO, as performance will be quick.

However, integrating the Payment Request API into a static HTML-based site is only part of the story; what about frameworks such as React, Svelte, Vue.js, or a lesser known one such as Ractive.js? There is increasing emphasis on using a framework to aid with construction of sites or online applications; thankfully the API can work with a wide range of frameworks that are used in today's web development.

To give you a flavor of what is possible, I've collated some example links that show how the API is used with some of the more popular frameworks:

- Angular

    The developer Hai Levi has created a wrapper for the Payment Request API – you can down the code from his GitHub site, at `https://github.com/sleekdevelopment/ng-payment-request-api`. If, as an Angular user, you plan to use Stripe as your PSP, then head over to `https://alligator.io/angular/stripe-elements/` – this has a good example of how to make use of the UI components provided by Stripe, with the Payment Request API and Angular.

- Vue.js

  Loris Leiva has a GitHub gist at `https://gist.github.com/lor isleiva/69e537202d35d4ccd1b4a5cb8ddecf1c`, which outlines a renderless Vue.js component for the Payment Request API. It focuses on the basic payment and returning of the outcome and so will likely need to be adapted to include the missing options such as `requestShipping`.

- React

  There are several examples available online – stripe has a component library set up for use with React, which you can download at `https://github.com/stripe/react-stripe-elements`.

  There are two React components that wrap the Payment Request API – one by Sara Vieira, which is available from `https://github.com/SaraVieira/react-payment-request`, and the other from Marco Lanaro; his GitHub site is at `https://lanaro.net/react-payment-request-api/`.

For those of you who have a keen interest in using React, we can see an example of the Payment Request in action – marco Lanaro has provided a working demo at `https://lanaro.net/react-payment-request-api/`, which is shown in Figure 7-1.

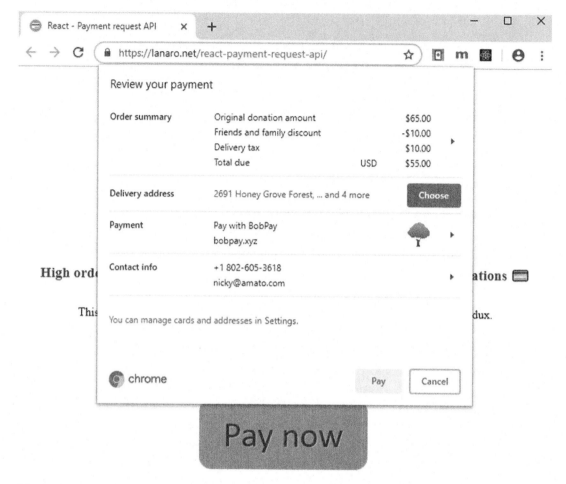

Figure 7-1. *A React implementation of the Payment Request API*

If you want to view it in action, you will need to use Chrome – it doesn't operate in Firefox.

His version was created as a higher-order component in React; this isn't strictly speaking a part of the React API, but an advanced pattern based around React's way of working.

It has all of the same type of detail that we've come to see throughout this book; it shows the right total, payment method, and so on. It's a good starting point for producing something in a React-based project – as long as we follow the same principles we've used thus far; we should be able to incorporate it into any React project where the API is needed.

If you would like to learn more about higher-order components in react, then head over to the React documentation at `https://reactjs.org/docs/higher-order-components.html`.

Choosing Our Framework

Now that we've seen an example of it working in a framework, it's time we took a look at what's coming up in this chapter – yes, we will work through an example using a framework, but surprise, surprise, it's not going to be React!

Yes, I thought I would throw that little sting into the mix: React is indeed incredibly popular. However, I've opted to go with a different framework – we're going to use Vue.js. There are two key reasons for this:

- The primary one is space available in this chapter – the amount of React code we need to create to get a store front running is substantial, whereas Vue.js can achieve it in less. We could easily write a whole book on just this part alone, so doing it any justice in 30 pages is already tough!

- This chapter isn't about how to build a site using framework X; it's about how we integrate the Payment Request API into said framework. Therefore, it doesn't really matter for the purposes of this book which framework we use; I prefer Vue.js as it is less bloated than some of the other frameworks, which makes it easier to integrate even a basic example of the API into the framework.

With this in mind, the shop we will be building will feature another all-time favorite food of mine: cookies! This would be perfect as a start point for a smaller outfit, particularly one who might deliver locally, but use a courier service for customers a little further away.

For the purposes of this little project, we're going to keep things simple – our shop front is too small to take on the likes of a major retailer, so making it complicated will not help our cause! When done, Figure 7-2 shows a screenshot of how our finished store will appear.

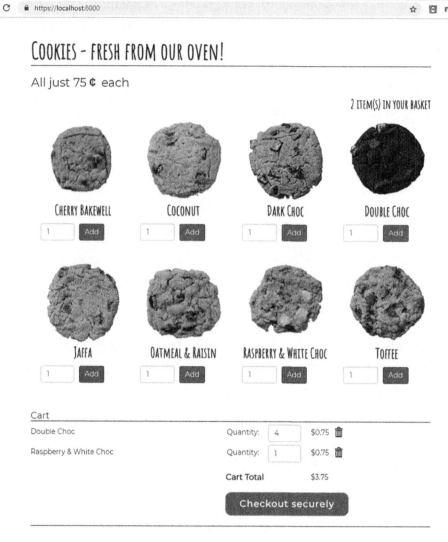

Figure 7-2. *The finished store front using Vue.js*

With this in mind, let's outline what we will cover in this chapter:

- We'll set up a basic store front to select cookies and add them to a basket.

- Our payment methods will be limited to basic-card and BobPay for this exercise.

- We'll make use of Bootstrap to display the basic layout.

- We'll include some shipping options – this to include choosing an address, setting suitable shipping options, and defaulting to free shipping if within half a mile of the store's location.

- We'll include some basic error handling and suitable feedback, so the customer knows if things have been successful or something has gone wrong with their purchase.

- We'll also take a look at where we might have to change our approach, to allow for any differences when using a framework such as Vue.js.

All of these are topics we've covered throughout the book, with the one exception – the defaulting to free shipping for orders nearby is a new addition. For this, we can use geolocation; it's a simple matter of comparing distance, and setting the appropriate delivery charge if the customer lives outside the 2-mile radius.

Okay – enough of the chitchat: it's time we got stuck into some real coding! Over the course of this chapter, we will work through constructing our cookie store; you will see similar principles in use to those we've already covered elsewhere in the book. We'll go through things in detail section by section, with particular emphasis on where things might differ when using a framework as an alternative to plain HTML markup. Our first point of call on this journey is the store front, so let's dive in and get this set up for use.

Creating the Store Front End

Although our store front looks different to the previous example, which we created back in Chapter 6, it nevertheless contains the same key elements that one might find on any shopping site – product gallery, totals, cart, add buttons, and of course our checkout button! In this instance, we'll be using Vue.js, so let's dive in and see what is required to get our store front operational.

SETTING UP THE STORE FRONT END

We have a fair amount of code to crack through and get set up, so let's make a start on setting up our store front:

1. We'll begin by creating a new folder called `cookies` in our project area – into this, extract the following files from the `cookies` folder that is in the code download which accompanies this book.

   - `fonts` folder

   - `css` folder

   - `images` folder

   - `index.html`

2. Next, create a subfolder at the root of the `cookies` folder – call this `js`, and extract the `bootstrap.min.js` and `vue.js` files from the code download into this folder.

3. With the basic markup in place, we can now turn our attention to adding in the Vue script to operate the gallery and cart. For this, go ahead and add the following code to a new document, saving it as `script.js` in the `js` subfolder. We'll go through it block by block, beginning with creating an array for our products:

```
const products = [
  {id: 1,title: 'Cherry Bakewell', price: 0.75, qty: 1, image: './
  images/cbakewell.png'},
  {id: 2,title: 'Coconut',price: 0.75, qty: 1,image: './images/
  coconut.png'},
  {id: 3,title: 'Dark Choc',price: 0.75,qty: 1,image: './images/dark-
  choc.png'},
  {id: 4,title: 'Double Choc',price: 0.75, qty: 1, image: './images/
  double-choc.png'},
  {id: 5,title: 'Jaffa', price: 0.75, qty: 1, image: './images/jaffa.
  png'},
  {id: 6,title: 'Oatmeal & Raisin',price: 0.75, qty: 1,image: './
  images/oatmeal-rasin.png'},
```

190

```
{id: 7,title: 'Raspberry & White Choc',price: 0.75,qty: 1,image: './
images/rasberry-white-choc.png'},
{id: 8,title: 'Toffee',price: 0.75, qty: 1, image: './images/toffee.
png'}
];
```

4. Next up is a helper function – `formatNumber` takes care of formatting the values in our cart with the correct decimal places and trailing zeros as needed:

```
function formatNumber(n, c, d, t){
  var c = isNaN(c = Math.abs(c)) ? 2 : c,
      d = d === undefined ? '.' : d,
      t = t === undefined ? ',' : t,
      s = n < 0 ? '-' : '',
      i = String(parseInt(n = Math.abs(Number(n) || 0).toFixed(c))),
      j = (j = i.length) > 3 ? j % 3 : 0;
  return s + (j ? i.substr(0, j) + t : '') + i.substr(j).replace
  (/(\d{3})(?=\d)/g, '$1' + t) + (c ? d + Math.abs(n - i).toFixed(c).
  slice(2) : '');
}
```

5. The next function is a Vue helper function, which calls `formatNumber`, to ensure prices and totals are displayed correctly:

```
Vue.filter('formatCurrency', function (value) {
  return formatNumber(value, 2, '.', ',');
});
```

6. The crux of our shopping cart is taken care of by the shopping cart component – inside of which we first define a property to render a total value for selected products and a method to remove items if needed:

```
Vue.component('shopping-cart', {
  props: ['items'],

  computed: {
    Total: function() {
      var total = 0;
      this.items.forEach(item => {
        total += (item.price * item.qty);
      });
```

```
      return total;
    }
  },

  methods: {
    removeItem(index) {
      this.items.splice(index, 1);
    }
  }
});
```

7. We then define a constant placeholder for our component and assign the key properties required to source the data needed for our component; we then set up a function to take care of adding items to our cart:

```
const vm = new Vue({
  el: '#app',

  data: {
    cartItems: [],
    items : products
  },

  methods: {
    checkout: function(event) {
      console.log("Checkout");
      initCheckout();
    },

    addToCart(itemToAdd) {
      var found = false;

      // Check if the item was already added to cart
      // If so them add it to the qty field
      this.cartItems.forEach(item => {
        if (item.id === itemToAdd.id) {
          found = true;
          item.qty += itemToAdd.qty;
        }
      });
```

```
            if (found === false) {
              this.cartItems.push(Vue.util.extend({}, itemToAdd));
            }

            itemToAdd.qty = 1;
          }
        }
      });
```

8. Our code is now complete – go ahead and save your work. Keep the `script.js`
    file open for now: we will continue with it shortly, in the next exercise.

At this point, we will now have a working store front that can be rendered – it won't
allow us to checkout, but it will at least permit us to add products into the cart and
generate the totals we will later use in the Payment Request API. The code behind this
store front is a little more complex than the previous example we created, so let's pause
for a few minutes and explore it in more detail.

Breaking Apart the Code

Over the last few years, I've worked with several frameworks, and written about one; a
key part of what attracts me to Vue.js is the simplicity of the markup. Sure, frameworks
such as React are popular, and serve their purposes, but one can't help but think – do
you really need *that* much code? I'm sure it's just a personal choice, but React does seem
somewhat code heavy at times...

But I digress – back to reality. If we take a look at the code behind our markup, you
will see much of it is standard HTML; we've also made use of Bootstrap to help with
styling the product gallery. We start with placeholders in place for data, such as the
number of items in our cart, at line 14. We then create a `container` <div>, inside of
which we render placeholder instances for each of the cookies that we have in our
store, by iterating through the products array created in `script.js`, using the `item in`
`items` method. This markup contains placeholders for the product image, `item.qty`,
description, and a call to initiate an `@click` event handler that adds the product to
the cart.

As an aside – you may have noticed that we've broken with tradition and included jQuery in this demo. This is purely to help with styling, as it's a requirement for Bootstrap – it's not used for the core basket and checkout code.

Moving on, the next block takes care of the shopping cart – it displays "Cart is empty" if `item.length` is true, that is, has zero items in the cart. As soon as we add items in, this is hidden, and each item is displayed as it is added into the cart. The markup is then rounded off by displaying the `check-out` div (containing the total) only when we have more than zero items in the cart, along with the Checkout securely button, ready for us to begin that part of the process. We then also display the `#instructions` block on completion of a successful transaction, to allow customers to add extra delivery details, should this be a production site!

If we turn our attention to `script.js` – let's take a quick look at how this code fits in: the code of interest starts at line 130. Here we define a products object array (and to which we've just referred to), before running the `formatNumber` helper function to ensure that all currency values are correctly formatted in code (with trailing zeros, etc.). This is referenced several times in the code, using the Vue filter at line 151.

Our main component starts at line 155 – inside this we define a computed method to work out the total cost of selected products and a `removeItem` method to take care of removing products as and when needed. We then bring all of this together by initiating an instance of Vue – this is where we assign the products array to the `items` property and create an `addToCart` event handler to drop products into our cart. However, the real magic kicks in at line 186 – this is where we call our instance of the Payment Request API, as our checkout cart...

Setting Up the Basic Checkout

Which is a perfect lead into our next exercise! If we were to preview the results from the previous exercise, we will see the cart appear; we can even add in products and get the relevant totals displayed. However, we won't be able to start the checkout process without updating our code – much of what we will cover in the next exercise should be somewhat familiar, as we've used versions of it already in earlier exercises.

This will be one of the first times we've pulled it together into a fully working example; the configuration of some of the elements will look different (such as delivery costs and methods), but it uses the same principles we've already covered throughout this book. Let's dive into our next exercise to see how we can configure the Payment Request API to operate with a Vue.js based site.

CONFIGURING OUR CHECKOUT

For this next exercise, we will do the editing in script.js, so make sure you have this open before continuing:

1. We'll start by entering a couple of blank lines at the top of the file. Go ahead and add in this constant, which will take care of defining the payment methods we will support via the site:

```
const methodData = [{
  supportedMethods: 'basic-card',
  data: {
    supportedNetworks: ['visa', 'mastercard', 'amex']
  }
}, {
  supportedMethods: 'https://bobpay.xyz/pay'
}, {
  supportedMethods: 'interledger'
}];
```

2. Next up, leave a line blank, then add in this function to manage rendering of any messages to the customer:

```
function displayMessage(symbol, status, mesg) {
  document.getElementById("message").classList.remove();
  document.getElementById("message").classList.add(status);
  document.getElementById("message").innerHTML = "<span>" + symbol +
  "</span>" + mesg;
}
```

3. This next larger function takes care of updating our instance of the Payment Request API, if a customer decides to select an alternative means of delivery; if the means chosen is invalid, a message is displayed on screen:

```
function updateDetails(details, shippingOption, resolve, stotal) {
  if (shippingOption === 'standard') {
    selectedOption = details.shippingOptions[0];
    otherOption = details.shippingOptions[1];
    details.total.amount.value = stotal;
  } else {
    selectedOption = details.shippingOptions[1];
    otherOption = details.shippingOptions[0];
    details.total.amount.value = (Number(stotal) + Number(3.99)).
    toFixed(2);
  }

  selectedOption.selected = true;
  otherOption.selected = false;
  details.displayItems.splice(1, 1, selectedOption);
  callback(details);
}
```

4. This next function is where we tie in everything together, define the values that will be shown on the checkout, and initiate our instance of the Payment Request API, before rendering it on screen:

```
function initCheckout (e) {
  if(window.PaymentRequest) {
    var subtotal = Number(document.querySelector(".cartamt").
    innerText);
    var delivery = 0.00;
    var beforetax = (subtotal + delivery)
    var tax = Number( beforetax * 0.0575);
    var total = Number(subtotal + tax + delivery).toFixed(2);

    const paymentDetails = {
      total: {
        label: 'Total due',
        amount: { currency: 'USD', value: total }
      },
```

```
displayItems: [{
  label: 'Sub-total',
  amount: { currency: 'USD', value: subtotal }
}, {
  label: 'FREE Delivery (3-5 days)',
  amount: { currency: 'USD', value: delivery.toFixed(2) }
}, {
  label: 'Sales Tax @ 5.75%',
  amount: { currency: 'USD', value: tax.toFixed(2) }
}],
  modifiers: [{
    supportedMethods: 'https://bobpay.xyz/pay',
    additionalDisplayItems: [{
      label: 'Processing fee',
      amount: { currency: 'USD', value: '3.00' }
    }],
    total: {
      label: 'Total to pay by card',
      amount: {currency: 'USD', value: Number(total +
      3).toFixed(2)}}
  }], shippingOptions: [{
    id: 'standard',
    label: 'FREE delivery (3-5 days)',
    amount: {currency: 'USD', value: '0.00'},
    selected: true,
  },
  {
    id: 'express',
    label: 'Express delivery (next day)',
    amount: {currency: 'USD', value: '3.99'},
  },
  ],
};
```

5. These next two variables that we declare take care of defining which details we need to ask for from the customer, such as shipping and email addresses:

```
const options = { requestPayerEmail: true, requestShipping: true };
const request = new PaymentRequest(methodData, paymentDetails,
options);
```

6. We now need to ensure that we respond to any changes in both the shipping address and method – for this, we fire either one of two event handlers:

```
request.addEventListener('shippingaddresschange', function(evt) {
  evt.updateWith(new Promise(function(resolve) {
    updateDetails(paymentDetails, request.shippingAddress, resolve,
    total);
  }));
});

request.addEventListener('shippingoptionchange', function(evt) {
  evt.updateWith(new Promise(function(resolve, reject) {
    updateDetails(paymentDetails, request.shippingOption, resolve,
    total);
  }));
});
```

7. The last function is where the magic really happens – its here where we determine if we can proceed (as there is at least one method of payment available) and whether this returns a successful result or failure:

```
if (request.canMakePayment) {
  request.canMakePayment().then(function(result) {
    if (result) {
      request.show().then(function(result) {
        result.complete('success').then(function() {
          displayMessage("\u2714", "success", "Payment received -
          thanks for your order!");

          const additionalDetailsContainer = document.getElementById('
          instructions');
          additionalDetailsContainer.style.display = 'block';
          additionalDetailsContainer.focus();
        });
```

```
        }).catch(function(err) {
          if (err.code == DOMException.ABORT_ERR) {
            console.error(err.message);
            displayMessage("&#128712;", "info", "Request has been
            cancelled.");
          } else {
            console.error(err.message);
            displayMessage("\u2716", "failure", "There was a problem
            with payment");
          }
        });
      } else {
        console.log('Cannot make payment');
        displayMessage("&#128712;", "info", "Sorry - no valid payment
        methods available");
      }
    }).catch(function(err) {
      console.log(request, err);
    });
  }
 }
}
```

Note   As per before, we're simulating the response back from what would be the payment method or PSP; in reality, this will take a few seconds to complete.

---

8. Go ahead and save your work – we can now preview the results: for this, fire up a Node.js terminal session, then change the working directory to the coffee folder.

9. At the prompt, enter this command and press Enter:

    ```
    ws --hostname localhost --https
    ```

    If we browse to `https://localhost:8000/`, we should now see the fruits of our labor, where our product gallery will display the cookies in all their glory!

Phew – we've rattled through the code at a fair pace; it might seem a lot, but most of it should now be familiar from the previous demos we've created from earlier in the book.

Dissecting the Code

If we take a look at the code we've created for our store, you might be surprised (or not?) that we've not had to make any allowances for using Vue.js – at all! This is one of the key attractions of using Vue.js: although our store front code is constructed differently, we're still able to use pretty much the same code as before for our back-end checkout.

We kick off with the same `methodData` constant that we've declared in previous demos; this stores the various payment methods available that are supported in our demo, such as `BobPay` or `basic-card`. This is then subsumed when we initiate our instance of the Payment Request API, later in the code.

Next up, we have two functions – the first, `displayMessage`, we've seen before; this handles the display of messages back to the customer, such as confirming a successful transaction. It's worth noting that although we're using Vue.js, the messages are displayed in the `#message` <div>, so we can reference this using vanilla JavaScript directly. The second function is `updateDetails`, which takes care of changes to the checkout, if we change the selected shipping address or delivery method. This might look different to previous examples, but this is purely because we've simplified the options available; we're still using the same principle of splicing in the updated option based on what has been selected by the customer.

Moving on, we have the `initCheckout` function – this operates in the same way as previous instances where we've specified details for our checkout, although we've specified different delivery methods for our customer in this demo. This time, though, the only change of importance is that the calling event is coming from the `methods` configuration property within our Vue.js instance.

The remaining functions (the two event listeners, `shippingoptionchange` and `shippingaddresschange`, and the `request.canMakePayment` block) are identical to previous instances that we've defined earlier in the book; there is no change required to allow these to operate in our demo.

Taking Things Further

At this point we should now have a working example of a checkout form – granted, it's not production ready yet, but it does show that we can make use of the Payment Request API within the context of a framework such as Vue.js.

This got me thinking though: how could we take things further, and experiment with the API? You may remember that at the end of Chapter 6, we touched on this with a few ideas; while researching for this book, two of those ideas struck a chord with me: geolocation and QR codes.

How might we implement such facilities within our checkout process? Well, as it happens, it's not that difficult to implement technically either of them, although the former will require you to sign up for a service – let's dive in and explore them in turn, beginning with adding geolocation support.

Case Study: Adding Geolocation Support

Geolocation, or to be more precise, geocoding, is the art of turning a human-readable address into longitude and latitude values, and has been around in various guises for years. It was not standardized though until 2008, with early examples of its use in browsers not appearing until Firefox 3.5, in early 2009.

As a standard today, it's supported by all of the major browsers – this makes it easier for us to implement, without the need to worry about providing fallback support. This then begs the question: how might we make use of it?

For our next demo, we're going to implement a proof of concept to see how far away our customer lives from our store. We can use this to work out if it might be quicker to get someone to walk or bike the goods to them rather than rely on the services of a courier company; the costs might be higher for the former, but you are paying for the privilege of a quick service! We will use the longitude and latitude of Apress' office in Spring Street, New York; our customer will live in an apartment a couple of blocks away in Varick Street.

Sounds simple enough? Well as it turns out, yes – and no: there is a lot more to it than just implementing geolocation from a technical perspective! The code we need to implement is not that complex, but there are a number of considerations we must factor in, around the logistics of how we implement such a feature. We'll cover these in more detail after the next demo, but we'll start with the biggest one first: who will provide the geolocation service?

Getting Prepared

The first consideration we need to allow for is the provision of the geolocation service – for this, we need to sign up to a service to use it; the most sensible option is to make use of the Geocoding API provided by Google.

To take part in this demo, you will need to sign up for an account with Google – they do provide a free trial version that is more than enough for the purposes of evaluating this technique. Google provide full instructions on how to do this at `https://developers.google.com/maps/documentation/geocoding/start`; you will need to do this to get the API key that needs to be inserted into the code provided within this demo. If you already have access to Google APIs and have a key that can be enabled for the Geocoding API, then this will work fine.

Note   Google asks for credit card details as part of activating the account; they will not charge until the end of the free period and will always ask for details before charging. As long as you cancel before the end of the trial, then there will be no costs incurred.

Creating Our Demo

Hopefully the use of Google hasn't put you off, and you've decided to take the plunge to try out this API – it opens up some interesting options, in addition to simply getting the latitude and longitude values for an address! We'll discuss some of these ideas after the exercise, but for now, let's dive in and see what is involved in more detail.

MAKING DELIVERY GEOLOCATION AWARE

Let's make a start with adding in our code:

1. We'll start by taking a copy of the `cookies` folder from the code download and saving it as `geolocate` in our project folder.

2. Next, we need to add in links to the Google geolocation script – for this, add in this line of code into `index.html`, immediately after the link to jQuery, on or around line 68:

   ```
   <script type="text/javascript" src="http://maps.googleapis.com/maps/
   api/js?key=YOUR API KEY"></script>
   ```

   …where YOUR API KEY will be the key provided by Google for your account.

3. Save the file then close it – we're done with editing that file.

4. Next, switch to `script.js` in your text editor, and add in some placeholder variables in at line 12 – these take care of the starting coordinates for our shop, the destination address, destination coordinates, and the calculated distance:

```
var CookiesShop_lat = 40.725605;
var CookiesShop_long = -74.0049139;
var destination, latitude, longitude, distance;
```

5. Next, leave a line blank then add in this function – this calls the geocode plug-in, into which we pass the destination address so it can calculate the latitude and longitude for us:

```
function GetLocation(dest) {
  var geocoder = new google.maps.Geocoder();
  geocoder.geocode({ 'address': dest }, function (results, status) {
    if (status == google.maps.GeocoderStatus.OK) {
      latitude = results[0].geometry.location.lat();
      longitude = results[0].geometry.location.lng();
      console.log("Latitude: " + latitude + "\nLongitude: " +
      longitude);
      distance = calcDistance(CookiesShop_lat, CookiesShop_long,
      latitude, longitude);
    } else {
      console.log("Request failed.");
    }
  });
};
```

6. Leave another line blank after the previous step, then add in this function – it calculates the distance between two pairs of latitude and longitude values:

```
function calcDistance(userLat, userLong, placeLat, placeLong) {
  //Earth Ray
  var R = 6371;
  //Get latlong value diferences between two points
  var dLat = (placeLat - userLat) * Math.PI / 180;
  var dLon = (placeLong - userLong) * Math.PI / 180;
```

```
//Calculate distance with Haversine Formula
var a = Math.sin(dLat / 2) * Math.sin(dLat / 2) + Math.cos(userLat *
Math.PI / 180) * Math.cos(placeLat * Math.PI / 180) * Math.sin(dLon
/ 2) * Math.sin(dLon / 2);
var c = 2 * Math.atan2(Math.sqrt(a), Math.sqrt(1 - a));
var distance = R * c;
return distance;
};
```

7. Scroll down to the start of the `updateDetails()` function – go ahead and add
    in these console log statements:

```
console.log(CookiesShop_lat + ", " + CookiesShop_long);
console.log(latitude + ", " + longitude);
console.log("Distance: " + distance);
```

8. We need to alter the conditions to determine which shipping method will be
    used – there are a number of changes in this next block, so to make it easier,
    we're going to replace the entire `paymentDetails` constant. Go ahead and
    delete lines 101 to 137, and replace it with this:

```
const paymentDetails = {
  total: {
    label: 'Total due',
    amount: { currency: 'USD', value: total }
  },
  displayItems: [{
    label: 'Sub-total',
    amount: { currency: 'USD', value: subtotal }
  }, {
    label: 'Standard shipping in US',
    amount: { currency: 'USD', value: delivery.toFixed(2) }
  }, {
    label: 'Sales Tax @ 5.75%',
    amount: { currency: 'USD', value: tax.toFixed(2) }
  }],
    modifiers: [{
      supportedMethods: 'https://bobpay.xyz/pay',
      additionalDisplayItems: [{
```

```
      label: 'Processing fee',
      amount: { currency: 'USD', value: '3.00' }
    }],
    total: {
      label: 'Total to pay by card',
      amount: {currency: 'USD', value: Number(total + 3).
      toFixed(2)}}
  }], shippingOptions: [{
    id: 'standard',
    label: 'Standard shipping in US',
    amount: {currency: 'USD', value: '3.00'},
    selected: true,
  },
  {
    id: 'express',
    label: 'Express delivery (next day)',
    amount: {currency: 'USD', value: '3.99'},
  },
 ],
};
```

9. Go ahead and save your work – we can now preview the results! For this, fire up a Node.js terminal session, then navigate to the geolocate folder we created back in step 1.

10. At the prompt, enter this command and press Enter:

```
ws --hostname localhost --https
```

11. Go ahead and browse to https://localhost:8000 when prompted – if all is well, we should see our checkout form appear once we've added some test products and hit the Checkout securely button. The form will look something similar to the screenshot shown in Figure 7-3, once we've selected the local address for delivery.

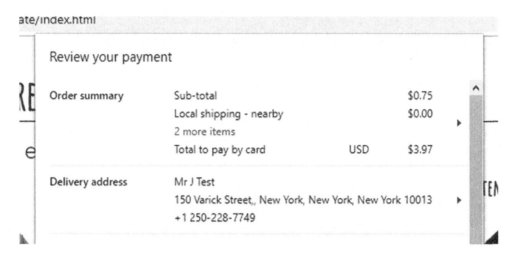

ate/index.html

Review your payment

Order summary	Sub-total		$0.75
	Local shipping - nearby		$0.00
	2 more items		
	Total to pay by card	USD	$3.97

Delivery address	Mr J Test
	150 Varick Street,, New York, New York, New York 10013
	+1 250-228-7749

Figure 7-3. *Displaying the checkout form, with the local address visible*

12. If we open up our developer console area, we should see some figures displayed – you may find it display "undefined" or "Request failed"; this is to be expected, but you should see something appear after 3-4 attempts (the results highlighted in red are the reason for showing the "Local shipping…" option).

```
DevTools - file:///C:/payment/geolocate/index.html        —   □   ×

    Elements   Console   Sources   Network   »        ⋮

 top                        ▼  ◉  Filter      All levels ▼   ⚙

  40.725605, -74.0049139                         script.js:53
  40.725774, -74.00555800000001                  script.js:54
  Distance: 0.057438174836206855                 script.js:55
  Request failed.                                script.js:25
  40.725605, -74.0049139                         script.js:53
  40.725774, -74.00555800000001                  script.js:54
  Distance: 0.057438174836206855                 script.js:55
  Latitude: 40.725774                            script.js:22
  Longitude: -74.00555800000001
>
```

Figure 7-4. *Proof that we're using location based on latitude and longitude values*

Although our demo isn't perfect, and that it does have a few wrinkles that need further work, it does show that we can make use of the basic principles of geolocation when working with the Request Payment API.

It's perfect for those occasions where we might offer free delivery if our customer lives within a certain radius. Or – how about putting a map or location details on the receipt, if local customers coming to collect goods need to know where you're based in town.

Leaving aside the potential uses for a moment (and we will come back to this shortly), we've covered some important techniques in our code, so let's take a moment to break it apart and explore it in more detail.

Breaking Apart Our Code

To implement a geocoding feature on our site required a few changes – we started by adding in a link to the Google Geocoding API script, before adding in several variables that hard-code our starting coordinates and provide placeholders for the destination location values. Next, we created a function that calls the Google Geocoding API; this turned the destination address of 50 Varick Street into numerical values that represent the location of our customer's home address.

We then used a somewhat complicated function to work out the distance between the two points, around a sphere – this is known as the Haversine formula. The reason for the reference to a sphere is that the Earth is circular; when we want to calculate the distances involved, we have to allow for the fact that we're effectively measuring around a sphere and not in a flat, straight line. We don't need to worry about the mechanics of how the function works – it's enough to know that as long as we provide valid references, then it will work out the distance for us.

The remaining changes to our code involve updating the `paymentDetails` constant, to allow for the addition of a local delivery option. We've included a few console.log statements as this is a proof of concept – you can see the raw information if you activate your browser's developer console.

Hopefully this has provided some food for thought – enabling a geolocation-based option opens the door to some interesting ideas that could work on any site. There are however a few things we need to consider though – let's pause for a moment to explore some of the logistics of what this technology means for our site.

If you would like to learn more about the Haversine formula, then Wikipedia has an interesting article at `https://en.wikipedia.org/wiki/Haversine_formula`.

What Next for Geolocation: Should We Use It?

It's a very good question – I suspect it may depend on how brave or disruptive you want to be! There are some benefits to using geolocation, although as with any service, it's important to bear in mind the costs involved.

If we were to use it, then the biggest two issues we face are that of privacy and cost – not only do we have an ongoing monetary cost involved, we should also get the customer's permission to use their location. However, the latter may not be so critical – we already ask the customer for their address during the checkout process; we take this a step further by converting it to suitable coordinates using client-side code. Granted, the address does have to be sent to the retailer (otherwise how can we ship the product!) – details of *how* we selected our shipping method remain client-side with the customer.

If we do decide to use this service, then what might we be able to do? Well, we could implement a map showing where the selected store is – what if that map also showed directions too? Assuming we make use of the geolocation (or Geocoding) APIs, then we can work out if it is quicker to get someone to walk or bike round to the customer – in a busy city, this would be a more effective means of transporting the goods rather than sitting in traffic!

There is a good reason therefore to charge something of a premium for this service – the person delivering the goods may not be able to get as many done as a standard courier service (as they have to go back to the store each time) but could get each run done quicker. This could potentially mean we could introduce a timeslot when the goods will appear – we can predict how long it is likely to take, if we limit the local delivery area to no more than say 2 miles from the store.

Ultimately it's all about simplicity and a little lateral thinking – the Payment Request API was designed to make checkout simpler and quicker to use; it's all about how we can make better use of the data available to use, so that customers know when to expect their delivery and plan their day around its expected time of arrival. Cast your mind back to the start of Chapter 4, where I made a reference to two companies with vastly different delivery services – now do you see what I mean about making the journey that much easier for customers?

Okay – let's move on: in the second of our two case studies, we're going to switch to implementing something that is particularly popular in Asian countries such as China or Japan. It's a really quick way of communicating information and can appear literally anywhere – anyone for a QR code?

Case Study: Using QR Codes

First invented back in 1994 for the Japanese automotive industry, QR codes are a great way to communicate short bits of information or addresses by simply scanning a matrix barcode. They can be seen everywhere – on the backs of buses, lorries, in catalogues, books, and the like; with the advent of the Internet, we can use them to direct customers to more extensive sources very easily.

In our case, there are several ways we could use QR codes – one might be to communicate a location map URL, or we might use it as a security check when collecting goods from a delivery point. In any case, they are really easy to add in: as we're already making use of jQuery to support Bootstrap, we can drop in a QR plug-in for this purpose.

For our next demo we're going to add in a simple QR code, using the plug-in by Jerome Etienne. We can download it from `https://github.com/jeromeetienne/jquery-qrcode`; it's a few years old but seems to work with the latest version of jQuery (3.4.1 at the time of writing).

Once you've downloaded it, it needs to be stored in the js subfolder under the geolocate folder; there is a copy available in the same folder in the code download as well.

We'll add in a simple address for now to illustrate how we might display the QR code, but this could easily be a link to a Google Map, or a security code used to confirm identity when collecting goods. Let's dive in and take a closer look at how we might implement this feature in more detail.

ADDING QR CODE SUPPORT

For this exercise, we will need to make changes in several places, so we'll start by opening `index.html` first, from within the geocode folder:

1. The first change we need to make is to add in our placeholder markup, so that we can position the QR code and some accompanying text: for this, go ahead and add the following immediately below the closing `</div>` of the `#instructions` block (which will be on or around line 62):

    ```
    <div id="qrcode">
    <p>Please scan for the location of your store:</p>
    <span class="code"></span>
    </div>
    ```

2. Next, switch to `script.js` and look for this line:

    ```
    displayMessage("\u2714", "success", "Payment received - thanks for
    your order!");
    ```

3. Leave a blank line, then add in the following code to generate our QR code:

    ```
    $('.code').qrcode({
      text: "234 Spring Street, New York",
      width: 128,
      height: 128
    });

    $("#qrcode > p").show();
    ```

4. The last change we need to make is to add some limited styling – drop the following code in at the end of `styles.css`:

    ```
    #qrcode { font-family: montserrat, sans-serif; float: right;
    margin-top: -265px; margin-right: 100px; }

    #qrcode > p { display: none; width: 180px; text-align: center; }

    .code { padding: 25px;}
    ```

5. Go ahead and save your work then close the files – we can now preview the results! For this, fire up a Node.js terminal session, then navigate to the geolocate folder we created back in step 1.

6. At the prompt, enter this command and press Enter:

    ```
    ws --hostname localhost --https
    ```

7. Go ahead and browse to `https://localhost:8000` when prompted – if all is well, we should see our checkout form appear once we've added some test products, then progressed through a test purchase. The form will look something similar to the screenshot shown in Figure 7-5, where we can see the QR code next to the extra instructions text field.

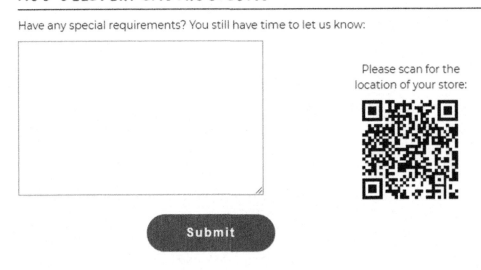

Figure 7-5. *The addition of our QR code*

This was an easy change to make – it adds something of a nice touch to the end of our checkout process! Although the code itself is very straightforward, let's take a moment or two to break it apart, so we can understand how it works in more detail.

Understanding How It Works

If someone asked us to add a QR code to their site, then we would be foolish not to use a plug-in for this purpose; creating one of these by hand would be a lengthy process! Although the plug-in we've used is a few years old, the basic principle hasn't changed – we feed in any information we like, and it converts it to a matrix-style barcode that can be scanned by any QR reader.

In our case, we start by setting up a suitable placeholder element in our markup for both the code and some accompanying text; we then call the `.qrcode` method on this element to render our selected text. It's worth noting that we've set both elements to only appear on a successful transaction; this is just to make sure they appear at the right time. The rest of the code simply styles the QR code, so it appears correctly within the extra information area, once a customer has completed a successful transaction.

Summary

One of the key strengths of the Payment Request API is its flexibility, and the ability to integrate it with multiple different frameworks. We may not see examples of how to achieve this online for a chosen framework – it doesn't mean it's not possible, just that people haven't posted their attempts online! That said, we've covered some useful tips on how to integrate the API with our chosen framework, so let's take a moment or two to review what we've covered in this chapter.

We kicked off by outlining a requirement to use a framework with the API, before exploring some of the options available and settling on our chosen framework, Vue. js. We then rapidly went through creating the store and initial back-end code, before exploring how we might take things further to help develop and refine the experience for our customers.

Next up came two example case studies – we mentioned about how we touched on one (implementing geolocation) briefly in the previous chapter, and the desire to explore how we might implement it in a practical sense. We then switched to taking a look at the use of QR codes and saw how they might be added to the site to help impart further information to the customer if this is appropriate and that they have a suitable QR reader available to them.

There is one more topic we should explore, before concluding our journey. The Payment Request API is part of a larger family of APIs, known as the Web Payment Handler API; this covers topics such as creating your own payment handler. No longer are we forced to have to use others; we have control! Hold onto your hats as we take a whistle-stop tour through the world of the Payment Handler API, in the next chapter.

CHAPTER 8

Project: The Future of the Web Payments API

Cast your mind back to Chapter 1 – remember where we talked about the main participants in an online transaction? One of those is the payment handler: you know this better as Google Pay, or perhaps Apple Pay. With their combined resources, I doubt there will be many of you who won't have seen at least one of these somewhere – either online or at your local store.

With enormous resources at their disposal, it's easy to understand how they have become so recognizable and why many will immediately mention their names if they were asked for the top two or three companies who offer this service. They are perfectly valid options and work well for those who already have accounts with either service. The question is though – what if we didn't want to use them and do something different…?

No problem: let me introduce you to the Payment Handler API! This API is a sister to the Payment Request API; both are part of the Web Payments family of open standards that are designed to help make online payments easier and more flexible (for both us and for our customers).

It's worth noting though that this flexibility does come at something of a price; the Payment Handler API is somewhat more complex than the Payment Request API and so more suited to being implemented once you have your e-commerce application up and running with the basic handlers in place. Don't let this put you off though – the API can offer some real tangible benefits; how about accepting Bitcoin or bank transfers, for example? Over the course of this chapter I'll take you on a whistle-stop tour of the API, so you can get a flavor of how it operates: let's start with understanding how this API fits in with the Payment Request API.

© Alex Libby 2019
A. Libby, *Checking Out with the Payment Request API*, https://doi.org/10.1007/978-1-4842-5184-3_8

What is the Payment Handler API?

Throughout this book, we've talked about the various aspects of the Payment Request API and how we can use it to create consistent carts that make the checkout process simple and fast for customers.

The Payment Request API is just one of several APIs that make up the Web Payments API, a family of open standards being developed to help make online payments easier for developers and customers alike. As it so happens, we've already touched on using two earlier in this book, in the form of the payment method identifier and the payment method manifest; together these all help determine how the various payment options we decide to support operate from within the Payment Request API.

So – what is the Handler API, and how does it fit into this mix? In a nutshell, it allows a web site to act as a payment handler, which (with the payment method identifier and manifest) we can integrate into the Payment Request API. It doesn't matter if this is the standardized method (which we know as "basic-card") or a third-party URL-based version such as Microsoft Pay; in each case, the handler is responsible for the following tasks:

- Making sure a payment can be made – this will vary depending on the payment method and the customer's payment request. For example, the customer may choose to pay by Mastercard, when the retailer only accepts Visa – in this case, the payment can't be made.

- If merchant validation is supported by the payment handler, respond to any merchant validation requests from the user agent.

- Verify that the information provided by the user results in a valid transaction – this process creates and returns a payment-specific object, which contains the information needed to handle the transaction.

From a customer perspective, all we see is a list of supported payment options; these names, or payment method identifiers, hide much of what happens when it comes to handling transactions! We touched on how these fit into the overall mix back in Chapter 1, but it's important to understand how the mix works, so let's quickly recap this in a little more detail.

Understanding the Mix

If you're like me, I suspect the only time you think about payments is when you have to get up and find your credit card for that online transaction, right? Or perhaps you use Google Pay and select this option instead?

Let's assume for a moment you've not embraced the likes of Google Pay (yet – at least) and that you prefer to use a credit card. Chances are, it will be either Visa or Mastercard who feature on the front – after all, who could hope to stand a chance against two of the world's most recognized brands when it comes to payments? (Just to put things in perspective: Visa is the world's seventh most valuable brand, and estimated to be worth $145 billion... yes you read right: $145 billion....)

With the advent of the Payment Handler API though, this could all change – other companies now have a chance to create and offer a similar service to the likes of Google Pay or Apple Pay; we're no longer tied to having to use standard credit or debit cards. For us as a developer, it means getting accustomed to some new concepts: we already touched on these in Chapter 1, but as a reminder, here are the two most important ones:

- Payment method identifiers – these are strings that identify the payment handler; they can be either the built-in methods to handle standard credit or debit cards (such as Mastercard or Visa), or URL-based (such as Google Pay). We can set a property to display a suitable title for the customer such as "Pay by credit card." At present, only one built-in identifier is available ("basic-card"), but others are under discussion.

You can learn more about the supported built-in methods at the W3C reference source at `https://www.w3.org/TR/payment-method-id/`.

- Payment handlers – this is the code required to interface between the payment method and our third-party payment provider. This might be a company such as Stripe or Square; they will handle processing of payments in the background and return an appropriate response to indicate success or failure of a transaction.

Over the course of this chapter, we're going to make use of these concepts to work through how we might create a payment handler for use in an e-commerce application. We've touched on using basic-card as one option, along with BobPay as

215

another – we're going to use the former as a basis for our own handler, as part of an extended demo. We need to start somewhere, so let's first take a look at the various elements that make up a payment handler in more detail.

Creating a Handler

At the time of writing this book, it was surprising how little information there is available on the subject of payment handlers – I suspect that with the API still to reach a ratified status, there is always a risk that features are added, changed, or removed, so documentation may become outdated. This said, one of the developers for Chromium, Rouslan Solomakhin, has created some useful examples of how we might build payment handlers; we'll reuse his basic-card example as the basis for our own version.

You can see his payment handler demos at `https://rsolomakhin.github.io/`.

When working with payment handlers, there are several files that are required, or locations that have to be provided; the exact number depends on whether we use the built-in basic-card method or a third-party payment app, such as Google Pay. The details of what we have to provide are listed in Table 8-1.

Table 8-1. *List of files or locations required for a payment handler*

Path	Contents
/	The root path of a web-based payment app that registers a service worker and a payment handler.
/manifest.json	A web app manifest that defines the web-based payment app.
/payment-manifest.json	A payment method manifest that defines how a payment method acts (this is required for third-party apps, not basic-card).
/installer.js	JavaScript code that handles a payment request.
/pay	A payment method identifier URL that returns an HTTP header pointing to the payment method manifest (required for third-party apps only).
/checkout	The actual checkout page exposed to users.

For our demo, we will create `installer.js` and `manifest.json` – the others are not needed, as they relate to payment handlers provided by third-party companies, which we're not using for this extended demo.

Getting Prepared

We're almost at a point where we can start coding, but before doing so, there are a couple of caveats we should keep in mind, when working through this demo:

- The Payment Handler API is still in a state of flux at the moment – documentation online on this is somewhat scarce and likely to become out of date, at least until the standard has become ratified. At the time of writing it has hit Candidate Recommendations status (April 2019); the latest version of the standard as published by the W3C is available at `https://www.w3.org/TR/payment-method-id/`.

- For the purposes of this book, we're going to keep things simple and reuse the standard basic-card identifier as the basis for our handler. However, this method is inherently insecure, as it transmits data in plain text; it is very likely not to remain the standard going forward. For now, we'll use it as a means to show how we might assemble a payment handler; things will almost certainly change once the Payment Handler API and Payment Request API are ratified as a mainstream standard.

Okay – enough chitchat: time to get stuck into coding! Before we do this, there are a couple of quick housekeeping tasks we need to complete first:

- We need a new folder in our project area – go ahead and create one called `basiccard`, saving it at the root of our project folder.

- We need a copy of the `basiccard - Completed version` folder that is in the code download that accompanies this book; make sure this is saved to the root of our project folder. We will make use of some prepared demo files from within it, when we come to test our handler later in this chapter.

- We will need a local web server to be running – for the purposes of this chapter, I will assume you've installed the local-web-server application we referenced back in Chapter 2. If not, go ahead and do so now; we'll cover the steps for running it later in this chapter.

With these steps out of the way, we can now start with coding! Our payment handler will be called CoffeePay – this is in homage to those web site owners who might put up donate buttons, or ask visitors to sub them a coffee as thanks for their work. It does also happen to be this author's favorite drink – given the themes used from earlier demos, it seems very appropriate too!

The first step in the process for building our handler is to define the payment identifier; in this instance though, we're going to do things slightly differently, so let's dive in and take a look at what this means for us in more detail.

Defining a Payment Method Identifier

When working with payment handlers, we have a few tasks involved – some easy, others much more complicated! It makes sense to start with something easy first: this will be the payment method identifier.

We've already seen these in action, although we've not dwelled on how they work in any great detail. Put simply, these tell the browser whether a manifest file is available at the defined URL; this tells the browser how the payment method should operate, as indicated in this example:

```
const request = new PaymentRequest([{
  supportedMethods: 'https://bobpay.xyz/pay'
}], {
  total: {
    label: 'total',
    amount: { value: '10', currency: 'USD' }
  }
});
```

In this case, we have `supportedMethods`, which is an obligatory property; this example also includes the total field, which isn't compulsory at this stage, and can be omitted. In all cases though, we don't actually make use of this configuration object until much later, during testing of our handler.

If you are using the `basic-card` method, then a URL is not needed; `basic-card` is built into the browser, so it is sufficient to simply specify basic-card as a value instead.

The browser sends a request to the URL, to determine if the manifest file exists – it will either receive 200 OK or error 204 (No Content); if something is returned, then it will look similar to this:

```
Link: <https://bobpay.xyz/payment-manifest.json>; rel=
"payment-method-manifest"
```

We must specify a URL that is secured (i.e. HTTPs), but it can be a fully qualified domain name or a relative path; either will work equally fine.

Building the Manifest

Once we've defined our payment method identifier, the next step is to create a payment manifest. This is a JSON file that resides on our web server and is used to define which payment apps can use this method. A typical manifest might look like this:

```
{
  "default_applications": ["https://coffeepay.xyz/manifest.json"],
  "supported_origins": [
    "https://coffeeandmore.com"
  ]
}
```

This JSON file uses two properties – the default_applications entry is an array of fully qualified URLs which point to manifests where the payment apps are hosted; this would reference the relevant JSON files for development, staging, and production usage.

We also have a supported_origins property in use – here we list all of the third-party payment apps which implement the same payment method. We touched on how multiple third-party payment apps can use the same payment method from earlier in the book; we can use * here to indicate that any origin can host the third-party app, but this reduces the security so isn't advisable.

The payment manifest that we're going to create will look different – as we're reusing a built-in standard one, we don't need to provide a payment method manifest; we instead need to provide a web app manifest. This works in a similar manner, using JSON – let's dive in and take a look in more detail.

CREATING A MANIFEST

The first stage in creating our payment handler is to define the name that appears when selecting a payment method – for this, run through the following steps:

1. We'll begin by opening a new document in your text editor – go ahead and add the following lines:

```
{
    "name": "Pay with CoffeePay",
    "icons": [{
        "src": "images/coffee.png",
        "sizes": "600x600",
        "type": "image/png"
    }]
}
```

2. Save this as `manifest.json` at the root of the `basiccard` folder, then close it – it does not need to be open for the remaining stages of this demo.

The first part of our handler is very simple – it's so simple that it hardly warrants any explanation! That said, all we do in this file is specify the name of our handler and the various icons we want to use. In our example, we've only specified one, but we might want to use a range of different sizes – for this, we might write something like this in place of the existing `icons` property:

```
"icons": [
  {
    "src": "images/manifest/icon-192x192.png",
    "sizes": "192x192",
    "type": "image/png"
  },
  {
    "src": "images/manifest/icon-512x512.png",
    "sizes": "512x512",
    "type": "image/png"
  }
],
```

We can see the effects of adding in an icon in the screenshot shown in Figure 8-1.

Figure 8-1. *Our payment manifest on display*

Okay – let's move on: the next stage in developing our payment handler is to create a payment app. This JSON-based configuration file contains some dummy data to initialize our service worker, with properties such as addressLine and country; in reality, we would select the required address when our checkout form is displayed. Let's take a look at the contents of this file in more detail.

Creating a Payment App

For the next stage of our extended demo, we're going to create a payment app, to hard-code details of a customer into the checkout form.

This will automatically pass properties such as their billing address, country, and credit card details – it is worth noting that we are doing this in a development capacity only and that I would absolutely **not** recommend doing this in a production environment! The basic-card format passes through unsecured data in plain text (such as the credit card number) – we're doing it here to illustrate how you might create a payment handler, but that in reality we should use one of the other methods of payment (such as token-based), which handles data far more securely.

This aside, setting up this app file is very straightforward – let's dive in and take a look:

CREATING THE APP

To set up the application, follow these simple steps:

1. We'll begin by creating a new file – save this as app.js at the root of the basiccard folder.

2. Add the following lines of code:

```
self.addEventListener('paymentrequest', (evt) => {
  evt.respondWith({
    methodName: 'basic-card',
    details: {
      billingAddress: {
        addressLine: [
          '1875 Explorer St #1000',
        ],
        city: 'Reston',
        country: 'US',
        dependentLocality: ",
        languageCode: ",
        organization: 'Google',
        phone: '+15555555555',
        postalCode: '20190',
        recipient: 'Jon Doe',
        region: 'VA',
        sortingCode: "
      },
      cardNumber: '4111111111111111',
      cardSecurityCode: '123',
      cardholderName: 'Jon Doe',
      expiryMonth: '01',
      expiryYear: '2020',
    },
  });
});
```

3. Go ahead and save then close the file – we don't need to keep it open for now.

Although this may look like a straightforward list of properties (such as `addressLine` and `country`), in reality, we wouldn't use this format: it's completely insecure and is only suited for development purposes. This said, it contains properties we've already used earlier in the book; we've put it into a format which means we don't have to specify them manually at the point of displaying our checkout form.

If you would like to learn more about the individual properties used, then MDN has a good list available at `https://developer.mozilla.org/en-US/docs/Web/API/PaymentAddress`. The properties listed in on that page are preceded with `PaymentAddress` – this part can be ignored (i.e. `PaymentAddress.postalCode` is the same as the `postalCode` entry listed in our demo). Okay – let's move on: up next is the real meat of our demo!

Installing the Payment Handler

Up until now, we've had it fairly easy – this is where things get a little more complicated! The real meat of setting up any payment handler will be in the installer; for this, we have to set up a service worker to help install and register our payment handler.

What is a service worker I hear some of you ask? Put simply, they are scripts that run in the background and open doors to features that don't need a web page. A good example would be to operate push notifications (you know, those annoying little notices that appear, pretending to be informational alerts, yet are anything but...), or we might use them to perform background synchronization for us.

If you would like to learn more, then Google has a useful article at `https://developers.google.com/web/fundamentals/primers/service-workers/`.

From a coding perspective, this is the most complex part of creating any handler – for our next exercise, we will work through creating one for our CoffeePay handler that will reuse the basic-card method we've already seen in action earlier in this book.

INSTALLING A SERVICE WORKER

The last stage of creating a payment handler is setting up the service worker and installer – this is a fairly substantial block of code, which we'll go through section by section. Let's make a start:

1. We'll start by opening a new file in your text editor – go ahead and save it as installer.js, at the root of the `basiccard` folder we created at the start of this chapter.

2. First go ahead and add in these helper functions – these take care of displaying or hiding messages on screen:

```
function showMessage(message) {
  const messageElement = document.getElementById('msg');
  messageElement.innerHTML = message + '\n' + messageElement.
  innerHTML;
}

function clearMessages() {
  document.getElementById('msg').innerHTML = ";
}

function showElement(id) {
  document.getElementById(id).style.display = 'block';
}

function hideElement(id) {
  document.getElementById(id).style.display = 'none';
}

function hideElements() {
  const elements = [
    'checking',
    'installed',
    'installing',
    'uninstalling',
    'not-installed',
  ];
```

```
    for (const id of elements) {
      hideElement(id);
    }
  }
}
```

3. Next, leave a blank line, then add in this function – this initiates a check to confirm if the payment handler is already installed and degrades gracefully if installation isn't supported:

```
function check() {
  clearMessages();
  hideElements();
  showElement('checking');

  if (!navigator.serviceWorker) {
    hideElement('checking');
    showMessage('No service worker capability in this browser.');
    return;
  }

  navigator.serviceWorker
    .getRegistration('app.js')
    .then(registration => {
      if (!registration) {
        hideElement('checking');
        showElement('not-installed');
        return;
      }
      document.getElementById('scope').innerHTML = registration.scope;
      if (!registration.paymentManager) {
        hideElement('checking');
        showElement('not-installed');
        showMessage(
          'No payment handler capability in this browser. Is chrome://
          flags/#service-worker-payment-apps enabled?',
        );
        return;
      }
```

```
    if (!registration.paymentManager.instruments) {
      hideElement('checking');
      showElement('not-installed');
      showMessage(
        'Payment handler is not fully implemented. Cannot set the
        instruments.',
      );
      return;
    }
    registration.paymentManager.instruments
      .has('instrument-key')
      .then(result => {
        if (!result) {
          hideElement('checking');
          showElement('not-installed');
          showMessage('No instruments found. Did installation
          fail?');
        } else {
          registration.paymentManager.instruments
            .get('instrument-key')
            .then(instrument => {
              document.getElementById('method').innerHTML =
                instrument.enabledMethods || instrument.method;
              document.getElementById('network').innerHTML =
                instrument.capabilities.supportedNetworks;
              document.getElementById('type').innerHTML =
                instrument.capabilities.supportedTypes;
              hideElement('checking');
              showElement('installed');
            })
            .catch(error => {
              hideElement('checking');
              showElement('not-installed');
              showMessage(error);
            });
        }
      });
  })
```

```
  .catch(error => {
    hideElement('checking');
    showElement('not-installed');
    showMessage(error);
  });
}
```

4. Next up comes the rather substantial `install()` function – this initiates the service worker we touched on earlier and displays suitable messaging to confirm if it is still installing or if installation has completed:

```
function install() {
  hideElements();
  showElement('installing');

  navigator.serviceWorker
    .register('app.js')
    .then(() => {
      return navigator.serviceWorker.ready;
    })
    .then(registration => {
      if (!registration.paymentManager) {
        hideElement('installing');
        showMessage(
          'No payment handler capability in this browser. Is chrome://
          flags/#service-worker-payment-apps enabled?',
        );
        return;
      }
      if (!registration.paymentManager.instruments) {
        hideElement('installing');
        showMessage(
          'Payment handler is not fully implemented. Cannot set the
          instruments.',
        );
        return;
      }
      registration.paymentManager.instruments
        .set('instrument-key', {
```

```
              name: 'Chrome uses name and icon from the web app manifest',
              enabledMethods: ['basic-card'],
              method: 'basic-card',
              capabilities: {
                supportedNetworks: ['visa'],
                supportedTypes: ['credit'],
              },
            })
            .then(() => {
              registration.paymentManager.instruments
                .get('instrument-key')
                .then(instrument => {
                  document.getElementById('scope').innerHTML =
                  registration.scope;
                  document.getElementById('method').innerHTML =
                    instrument.enabledMethods || instrument.method;
                  document.getElementById('network').innerHTML =
                    instrument.capabilities.supportedNetworks;
                  document.getElementById('type').innerHTML =
                    instrument.capabilities.supportedTypes;
                  hideElement('installing');
                  showElement('installed');
                })
                .catch(error => {
                  hideElement('installing');
                  showMessage(error);
                });
            })
            .catch(error => {
              hideElement('installing');
              showMessage(error);
            });
        })
        .catch(error => {
          hideElement('installing');
          showMessage(error);
        });
    }
```

5. As with all good software, we need to provide an uninstall option too; for this, leave a line, then add in the following code:

```
function uninstall() {
  hideElements();
  showElement('uninstalling');

  navigator.serviceWorker
    .getRegistration('app.js')
    .then(registration => {
      registration
        .unregister()
        .then(result => {
          if (result) {
            hideElement('uninstalling');
            showElement('not-installed');
          } else {
            hideElement('uninstalling');
            showElement('installed');
            showMessage(
              'Service worker unregistration returned "false", which
              indicates that it failed.',
            );
          }
        })
        .catch(error => {
          hideElement('uninstalling');
          showMessage(error);
        });
    })
    .catch(error => {
      hideElement('uninstalling');
      showMessage(error);
    });
}
```

6. We finish with a single one-liner – add in this add the end of the file to initiate our service worker:

```
check();
```

7. Go ahead and save the file – we'll keep it open for the moment, as part of reviewing the code in a moment.

Yikes – that was indeed a substantial piece of coding! If you got to this stage, then congratulations: you deserve a break. It contains some useful key principles that we will no doubt use or see when creating payment handlers; it's worth reviewing the code in more detail. Before we do this though, take a few moments to catch your breath and get a drink – when you're good to go, let's take a look at that code in more detail.

Dissecting Our Code

Although we've covered a lot of code while creating our CoffeePay handler, the great thing about payment handlers is that we don't have to worry about how the front end appears to the customer or how it works. Instead, we can absolutely focus on the back-end functionality – everything we need can be accomplished using plain JavaScript, without the need for any external libraries. Let's take a look in more detail:

The bulk of the code we created sits in installer.js – we started by creating some helper functions to control how messages displayed back to the customer are rendered on screen. This includes defining all of the various states of install, such as checking, not installed, or uninstalling. Most of these you will not have seen in action in our demo, but that is purely because we are working locally; on a web site where there will be a delay in response, these states will be more visible.

Next up came the check() function – this performs a check to ensure our browser can support payment handlers, or their installation using service workers. It's worth noting that the code at lines 50-58 could potentially be removed; this relates to a specific check for Chrome. Chrome has had native support for the Payment Request API since September 2017; given it's propensity to update frequently, there is a good chance that this check could now be redundant for many Chrome users!

I say potentially though, as this code can also be triggered by Firefox Developer Edition too – a check in your site's analytics will confirm if this browser is being used and whether it is safe to remove this check.

The next function is where the real magic happens – `install()`. Inside this we perform similar checks to ensure that payment handlers can be supported or that the payment instruments can be installed correctly; provided these checks are successful, it will install the handler for us or display a suitable error if installation has failed. We then complete the code with the uninstall function, which de-registers and uninstalls the handler for us; the `check()` call at the end initiates the whole process.

Okay – let's change tack: now that we've worked our way through a proof of concept example of how a payment handler might work, it's a good opportunity to consider the wider picture, and not just the technical innards of creating handlers!

What do I mean by this? Well, throughout all of our demos to date, we've always displayed the checkout sheet, where we can select which payment method to use, the address detail, and so on. What if we could *actually* skip this sheet?

Streamlining the Process

I have a confession to make – when researching for this book, I (against my better judgement) felt we should broach the subject of "best practice." Why "against my better judgement" though? Surely this is what we should always strive for, right?

Yes, it is true that we should always look to follow "best practice" where it is relevant. However, when anyone mentions those words, I must admit it makes me cringe – I frequently think "oh no, not again!"

There's a good reason for this: I hear and see far too many instances where people claim something is "best practice," yet it is clear that this isn't always the case! It's for this reason I am reminded of the curse of the "Scottish Play" – where an actor does not utter the name of a particular play, for fear of instilling a curse on their show. This is why I try to avoid uttering those words where possible...

If you've not heard of this play, then take a look at `https://en.wikipedia.org/wiki/The_Scottish_Play` – it explains what the real name of this play is and the history behind why one should never refer to it by that name.

But I digress. I know people strive to make sure that their implementation follows best practice where possible (and there is nothing wrong with that concept), but how do we *really* define what is "best practice"? Isn't it more a case of streamlining or optimizing our process, at least in part? For me, it should not be about blindly following what others do – each solution is different, and I would maintain that as long as it includes the right features that have been tested, we should focus on optimizing it for our customers.

One way to achieve this is to streamline what is displayed – Ian Jacobs from the W3C posted a blog article on two ideas that are being considered: just-in-time registration, and skipping the sheet. These take a little explaining, so let's start with just-in-time registration and see what this means in practice.

The idea of just-in-time registration process is designed to handle those instances where browsers display payment handlers which are based on payment methods that are accepted by the merchant's web site. Normally customers have to manually install each handler, but the W3C proposes to allow automatic registration via use of an authorization code and appropriate payment method manifest.

The second relates to instances where we can skip over the display of the initial payment sheet – that is, go past the screen where we might select a payment method, or specify a delivery address. For this to happen, there are certain conditions that have to be met:

- The merchant detects that support for only one payment method, and it is a URL-based method (i.e. not basic-card).

- The merchant doesn't require information to be entered (such as shipping address).

- The customer has said payment handler already installed, or can install it via just-in-time registration.

If the preceding conditions can be met, then at the point of initiating the checkout form (e.g., by clicking "Buy"), the initial page will be skipped.

If you would like to learn more, then the original W3C blog article is available at `https://www.w3.org/blog/wpwg/2018/08/20/further-streamlining-the-payment-request-user-experience/` – please bear in mind though that certain elements of the API are still in a state of flux, so features may change before the API becomes a ratified standard.

Okay – having considered what we should implement as "best practice" (grr....), now is an opportune moment to reflect on the wider issue of security around payment handlers. Payment handlers are by their very nature a very powerful tool; for some it is understandably scary as to just how much power they can wield from a standard browser! With that in mind, let's explore some of the security concerns that we might have, and how these can be mitigated when using payment handlers.

Considering Security Implications

Payment handlers are indeed a powerful tool – when used correctly, we have the ability to really streamline the checkout process for our customers. This of course will bring up security concerns; how these are managed will differ between browser vendors.

As an example, Chrome (who were first to ship support), implemented a range of checks and prevention measures, which include.

- Ensuring that payment handlers only operate in an SSL-secured environment.

- Disallowing communication with handlers if their security state is listed as red or grey on the BadSSL web site (`https://badssl.com`).

- Hiding payment handlers if their origin is listed as unsafe in Google's lists of unsafe web sites (which can be queried using Google's Safe Browsing API).

The exception to this is localhost – this will permit handlers to work in an HTTP and HTTPS environment, for development purposes only.

Google also limits payment handler functionality, by running it in its own "sandboxed" environment in the browser; this keeps it separate to the main browser process. It will also block any content, requests, or scripts that are not secured and that originate from a cross-domain source. Chrome though has given access to some additional settings that control payment handler behavior, such as whether we can skip the payment sheet (or screen) before launching the handler, block handlers from a given origin (such as ones we don't want to support), or prevent customers from registering a handler during the payment process.

From a customer perspective though, we need to be mindful of whether the option to enable payment handlers has been enabled in the browser, and if so, what details are stored within the browser. Chrome has enabled the option to store details by default since version 68 (mid-2018), so customers may not automatically realize this is the case. The setting can be disabled, but the trade-off is that we should provide a fallback mechanism, at least until the Payment Request API (and handlers) becomes an accepted mainstream standard.

Ultimately though the Payment Handler (and Payment Request) API is all about making it easier to purchase online; we can help customers by evangelizing the benefits of a quick checkout, ensuring our site is fully protected, using reputable third-party services, thoroughly testing our site, and helping with support FAQs (particularly if we're implementing the API into an existing site). We can't stop customers from doing something silly, but as long as we can help identify, educate, and minimize risk, this will help encourage adoption of this new standard into mainstream use.

As an aside, a new 3D Secure security standard is due to come into force in Europe – you can learn more about how this will affect the Payment Handler API, from the W3C blog at `https://www.w3.org/blog/wpwg/2018/01/26/a-crisper-picture-of-3d-secure-2-and-payment-request/`.

Testing Our Payment Handler

At this stage, we should have a working handler – it's time to test it! For this, we'll do the testing in two parts: the first will use a restyled version of Rouslan Solomakhin's original demo.

The second will revisit one of our earlier demos, to see how the payment handler might perform in a more realistic environment, where we may elect to do things such as changing the shipping type or even the destination address. Let's start with confirming that our handler actually works first, using Rouslan's (restyled) demo.

TESTING THE HANDLER – PART 1

For this last exercise, we'll make use of the CoffeePay handler we've just created – we will focus more on making sure it works rather than delving into building our test page. With this in mind, let's crack on:

1. We'll begin with firing up a Node.js terminal session – once running, change the working folder to be the basiccard folder we set up in the previous exercise; this has both the main code and testing page already set up.

2. At the prompt, enter this command, and press Enter:

    ```
    ws --hostname localhost --https
    ```

3. Go ahead and browse to https://localhost:8000 in Chrome; if all is well, you should see the page shown in Figure 8-2.

 # Payment Handler for "CoffeePay"

This is a simple payment handler for "CoffeePay". It does not open a window for user interaction.

The payment handler is not installed | **Verify**.

Install

View the source code:

- Installer
- App
- Web app manifest

Figure 8-2. Our new payment handler, ready to install

4. Click the Install button – after a couple of moments, you will see a confirmation that CoffeePay has been installed; it will show the scope, as well as the supported payment method (Figure 8-3).

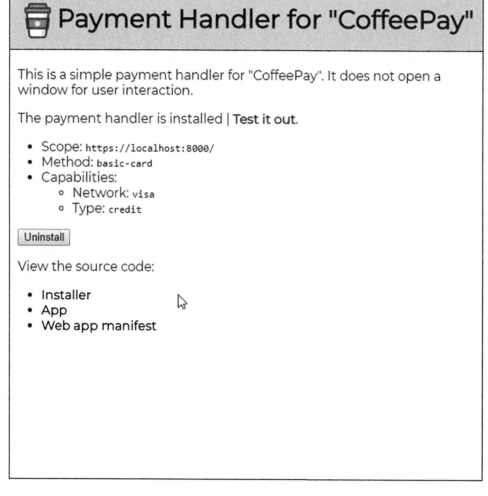

Figure 8-3. *Testing our new payment handler*

5. Now click the Test it out link shown on the page; you will see our preconfigured test page appear, as indicated in Figure 8-4.

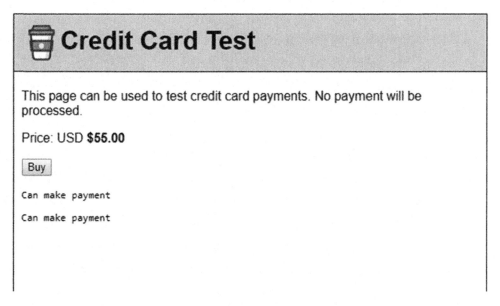

Figure 8-4. *The test page for our payment handler*

6. Click the Buy button – you will notice that we've not asked for any contact details; these have already been provided earlier, when we set up the payment app. You will see something akin to the screenshot shown in Figure 8-5.

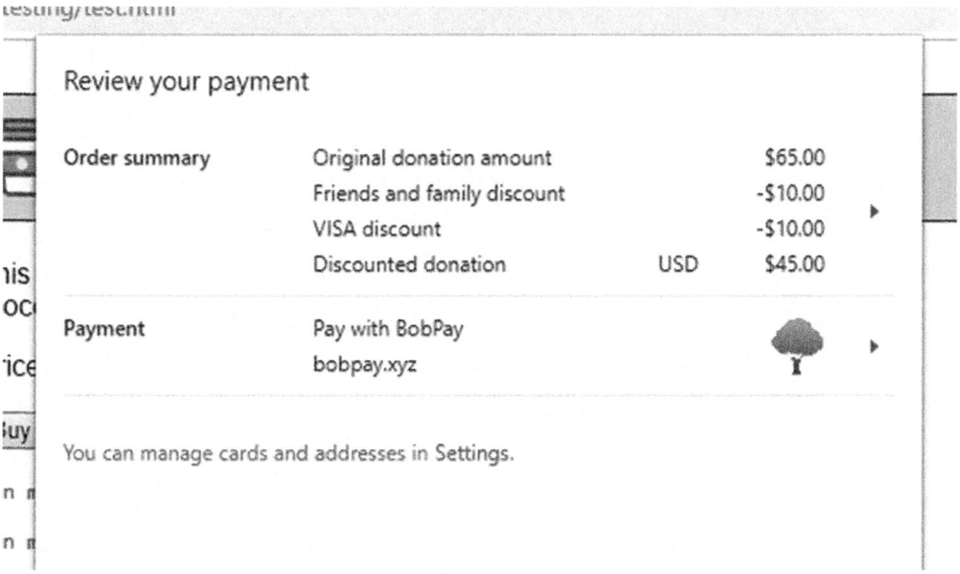

Figure 8-5. *Testing our payment handler*

7. You may see a different handler present – if you do, don't worry: click the arrow to the right, to select our newly created payment handler (Figure 8-6).

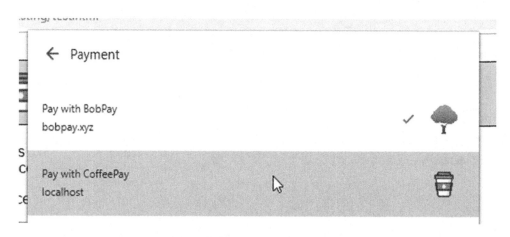

Figure 8-6. *Our new payment handler, in all its glory*

8. Back on the previous page, go ahead and select Pay – you'll see the (by now familiar) processing spinner; it will then display a simulated response, with our client details listed on the page (an extract of which is shown in Figure 8-7).

This is a demo website - no payment will be processed.

Response from the server:

```
{
  "requestId": "ac286387-859e-490e-80e1-fc1fe1bd8eb7",
  "methodName": "basic-card",
  "details": {
    "billingAddress": {
      "addressLine": [
        "1875 Explorer St #1000"
      ],
      "city": "Reston",
      "country": "US",
      "dependentLocality": "",
      "languageCode": "",
      "organization": "Google",
      "phone": "+15555555555",
      "postalCode": "20190",
      "recipient": "Jon Doe",
      "region": "VA",
      "sortingCode": ""
    },
    "cardNumber": "4111111111111111",
    "cardSecurityCode": "123",
    "cardholderName": "Jon Doe",
    "expiryMonth": "01",
    "expiryYear": "2020"
  },
  "shippingAddress": null,
  "shippingOption": null,
  "payerName": null,
  "payerEmail": null,
  "payerPhone": null
}
```

Figure 8-7. *An extract of the simulated response*

So far, we've tested our handler in a simulated example; what about a more realistic example? While it wouldn't be wise to put our handler out into a real-live site (at least just yet), we can at least test in a more complete demo – let's do that as part of our next exercise:

TESTING THE HANDLER – PART 2

The real proof of it working lies in using one of our previous demos – for this, follow these steps:

1. We'll use the `cookies` demo from Chapter 7 – first, fire up a Node.js terminal session, then change the working folder to the cookies folder inside our project area.

2. At the prompt, enter this command and press Enter:

    ```
    ws --hostname localhost --https
    ```

3. Next, browse to `https://localhost:8000`; and click Add against a couple of cookies – the exact number isn't critical for this demo.

4. Go ahead and hit Checkout securely, to begin the checkout process.

5. Our next step is the moment of truth: click the arrow to the right of the payment method, and make sure Pay with CoffeePay is selected, if this isn't already showing (Figure 8-8).

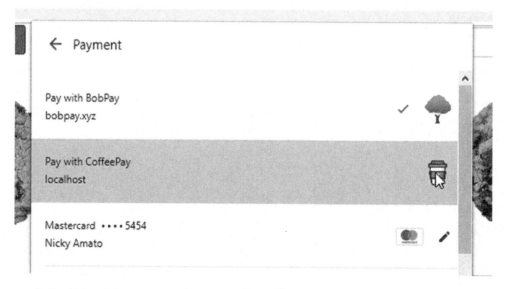

Figure 8-8. *Selecting our new payment handler*

6. On the previous screen, hit Pay – if all is working OK, we should see our confirmatory message appear and disappear after a short while, as indicated in Figure 8-9.

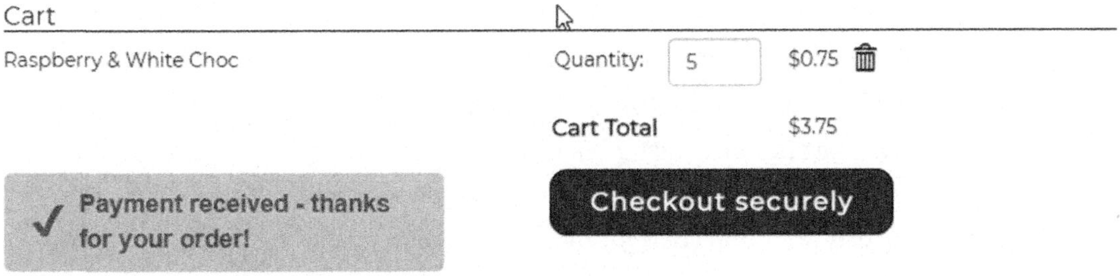

Figure 8-9. *Confirmation that our handler has worked*

We now have a working proof of concept that hopefully gives you a flavor of how payment handlers work – we've covered some useful tips, so let's relax for a moment, grab a drink, and take a closer look at the code in more detail.

Dissecting the Code

Fire up your text editor, and take a look at these three files from the testing folder in the `basiccard` demo: `test.html`, `merchant.js,` and `util.js`. At first glance, you might be forgiven for thinking that it looks nothing like what we've done before, right? In some respects, this is true; but as someone once said to me, "you're looking, but you're not seeing...."

Okay, I confess: perhaps I should explain what I mean by that somewhat cryptic comment! The truth of the matter is that we don't have to follow a rigid set pattern or use the same code when creating payment handlers or initiating the Payment Request API; as long as we follow certain principles then we can code them as we wish. In our case, the code may *look* different, but we're using the same principles such as displaying the form (`request.show()`), creating our supported instruments (`supportedInstruments = [...]`), and `canMakePayment()`. These are all methods or terms we've met earlier in the book, but implemented slightly differently.

This is one of the great things about the Payment Request API, or even the Payment Handler API; neither requires external libraries and so can use standard JavaScript techniques to implement the API as we see fit.

We started with a basic HTML markup page (`test.html`), which we use to initiate an instance of our checkout form using the Payment Request API; this calls `onBuyClicked()` to first confirm if the API is supported, before initiating our checkout form if the answer is positive. The initiation is taken care of by the `buildPaymentRequest()` call at line 145 (just before the `onBuyClicked()` function); we first perform another check to ensure we can support the API, before defining objects as placeholders for our supported payment methods (lines 13-17), and build the transaction details (lines 19-61). This transaction detail block includes the standard cost, plus taxes, and a discount.

The final stage is to fire up our checkout form, which we do from line 115; we first confirm that we have at least one valid method of payment available. We then check to see if there have been any changes to the payment method (if there has, we update the selected payment method from line 127), before using the done function at line 73 in `util.js`, to return a response which lists the results of our transaction.

Summary

Over the course of this book, we've covered a host of interesting concepts around the Payment Request API and how implementing it could really turn online payments on its head. The same applies to creating payment handlers; we've explored some useful techniques in this chapter, so let's take a moment to review what we have learnt.

We kicked off with introducing the new Payment Handler API and saw how it plays a key role in the checkout process; we then covered off how the Handler API fits in with the other key elements that make up the Payment Request API.

Next up, we then moved onto creating a proof-of-concept handler, using code based around the basic-card handler; we covered topics such as defining our payment method identifier, to building the manifest and creating the installer for our handler.

We then moved onto exploring how we might streamline the process and discussed a little on the wider topic of security; this was to understand some of the key areas of concern rather than just focus on the technical innards of our code. We then rounded out the chapter with a two-part demo to test the new handler, both in a limited environment and using one of the existing demos we created from earlier in the book.

All good things must eventually come to a close, as we reach the end of this book; I hope you've enjoyed our adventure through the world of the Payment Request API as I have writing this book, and that this will see you begin to embrace a new API that promises to disrupt the whole market around checkout forms in modern browsers.

APPENDIX

API Reference

API Interfaces

Interface	Purpose
MerchantValidationEvent	This enables a merchant to validate themselves as being allowed to use a particular payment handler, such as Apple Pay.
PaymentAddress	An object that contains address information, such as billing and shipping addresses.
PaymentMethodChangeEvent	This describes the paymentmethodchange event which is fired by some payment handlers, if a user changes their chosen payment instrument, such as switching from Apple Pay to using a store card.
PaymentRequest	This is the primary access point for the API, and lets web-enabled content and applications accept payments from customers/visitors.
PaymentRequestEvent	This event is sent to a payment handler when a PaymentRequest has been made.
PaymentRequestUpdateEvent	This enables the API to update the details of a PaymentRequest object in response to a user action, such as changing the chosen shipping method.
PaymentResponse	This is returned when a user has selected a payment method and approves a payment request using the API.

For a complete list of individual properties for each interface, please refer to https://developer.mozilla.org/en-US/docs/Web/API/Payment_Request_API#Interfaces.

243

© Alex Libby 2019
A. Libby, *Checking Out with the Payment Request API*, https://doi.org/10.1007/978-1-4842-5184-3

API Properties

API property	Purpose
`HTMLIFrameElement.` `allowPaymentRequest`	This Boolean-based value indicates whether the Payment Request API can be invoked on a cross-origin iframe.

```
https://developer.mozilla.org/en-US/docs/Web/API/HTMLIFrameElement/
allowPaymentRequest
```

API Events

These events are delivered by the Request Payment API to a PaymentRequest object when users make a change to their personal information in the course of filling out a checkout form:

Event	Purpose of event
`merchantvalidation`	This requires the merchant to validate itself as being allowed to use the payment handler.
`payerdetailchange`	This event handler should be set to check the values in each field to ensure they are valid and display error messages if fields contain invalid information. Once updated, the retry() method needs to be called to update any invalid entries.
`paymentmethodchange`	This is fired when users change the selected payment method within a given payment handler, such as from credit card to Google Pay.
`shippingaddresschange`	This is triggered when a customer changes the selected shopping address, including adding a new address for the first time.
`shippingoptionchange`	This is fired when the selected delivery option is changed by the customer - as an example, this might be from standard 3-5 day delivery, to express next day, if the customer wants it delivered sooner.

Useful References

- Mozilla Developer Network has some useful information on the API, which is available at `https://developer.mozilla.org/en-US/docs/Web/API/Payment_Request_API`.

Index

A, B

AbortError() function, 107

Application program interface (API)

    autofill options, 2

    benefits of, 4, 5

    events, 244

    interfaces, 243

    misconceptions, 5, 6

    object flow, 62

    payment request, 2, 3

    properties, 244

    references, 244

    terminology, 7–10

    Web payments standard, 7

C, D

Checkout form configuration, 63

    change order folder

        details, 73

        displayItems function, 74

        exploring form, 75

        payment.js, 73

        steps, 72

        updated form, 74

        view items, 72

    code details, 69, 70

    display icon, 63

    gift cards and discounts

        amount.addEventListener event

            handler, 76

        applying discount, 78

        code details, 79

        displayItems block, 77

        index.html, 76

        promotion code, 75

        steps, 76

    handling multiple currencies, 65

    screenshot, 70–72

Configuration

    payment method

        local web server, 60

        paymentDetails array object, 58

        paymentMethods object, 57

        paymentOptions variable, 59

        set up, 55, 56

        testing, 61

        window.onload() function, 57

        working process, 61, 62

    payment process

        customer details, 80–82

        iframe support, 82–84

        options folder, 81

        payment.js, 81

        updated options, 81

E

Error handling

    amount.addEventListener()

        function, 39

    canMakePayment() function, 45

Printed in Great Britain
by Amazon

46717427R00150